An Inspirational Tour of the Forbidden City

魂 游 故 宫

Illustrator: Yang Zi
Managing Editor: Lan Peijin
Translator: Zhang Shaoning
English Editor: Yu Ling
Designer: Yuan Qing et al.
Cover Designer: Lan Peijin

First Edition 2005

An Inspirational Tour of the Forbidden City

ISBN 7-119-03900-8

© Foreign Languages Press

Published by Foreign Languages Press
24 Baiwanzhuang Road, Beijing 100037, China
Home Page: http://www.flp.com.cn
E-mail Addresses: info@flp.com.cn
　　　　　　　　　sales@flp.com.cn

Distributed by China International Book Trading Corporation
35 Chegongzhuang Xilu, Beijing, 100044, China
P.O. Box 399, Beijing, China

Printed in the People's Republic of China

An Inspirational Tour of the Forbidden City

魂 游 故 宫

Foreign Languages Press
外 文 出 版 社

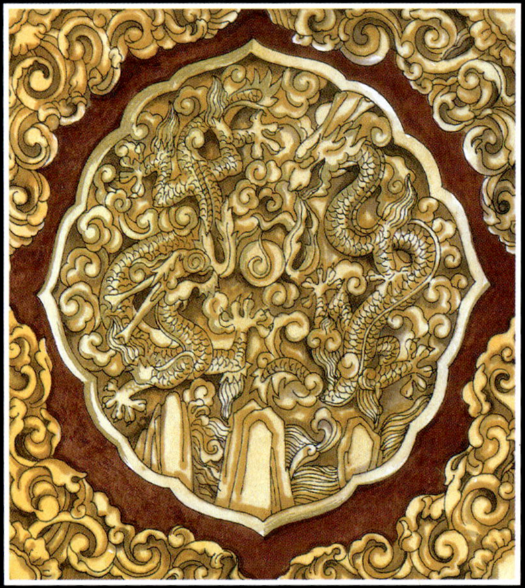

The Forbidden City in My Heart

The ancient Chinese astronomers divided the sky, with the Polestar as the center, into three enclosures and 28 constellations. The former include the Purple Forbidden, Supreme Palace and Heavenly Market enclosures. The Purple Forbidden Enclosure covers the region around the Polestar. The ancient Chinese believed that it was fixed in the sky as a center around which all stars rotate. Therefore, the Polestar was called the Emperor Star, and the Purple Forbidden Enclosure was believed to be the place where the Heavenly Emperor lived.

Since the emperors on earth were believed to be the sons of Heaven, their palace was called the Forbidden City.

Although the Forbidden City on earth is not as distant as the court in Heaven, the word "forbidden" hints at inaccessibility to ordinary people.

From far away they could see the red walls and golden tiles, but they were not allowed to go near it, when even a small bird or insect was free to go in and out of it. The 10-m-high walls and 52-m-wide moat around the mysterious Forbidden City blocked the prying of curious eyes.

The people looked at it from a distance on the other side of the moat, talked about it outside the walls, imagined what the inside was like, and dreamed of it, while the small birds and insects saw it with their own eyes and even experienced it.

They wished they could ask the birds and insects what they had seen.

Is the Emperor awesome?
Is the Empress beautiful?
Are the palace women miserable?
Are the eunuchs vicious?

It is said that during the reign of Emperor Yongle (1043-1424), two incidents occurred within the imperial palace, resulting in the executions of 3,000 imperial concubines and palace women. The emperor was present on the execution ground, watching with pleasure how the delicate women were tortured to death. What kind of life had the poor women led within the walls of the Forbidden City?

Emperor Jiaqing (reigned 1796-1820), obsessed with Taoist superstition, devoted himself to making "pills of immortality with the bodies of palace women." Sixteen palace maids tried to strangle him, but failed. They, plus two imperial concubines who were implicated, were executed by being cut into pieces alive. The emperor, having narrowly escaped death, was too afraid to live in the palace any more, believing that "there must live the revengeful ghosts of the wronged." Twenty years later, he returned to the Forbidden City, not without trepidation, only to die on the first night. Was he killed by the avenging ghosts of the maids?

In the last year of Ming Emperor Chongzhen's reign (1628-1644), when peasant rebels led by Li Zicheng broke into Beijing, the desperate emperor killed the empress and princesses with his sword. When the screams and chaos died away, mutilated corpses littered the great hall among pools of blood. The emperor then hanged himself from a tree on nearby Jingshan Hill. Later, it was said that "on an overcast day the wailing of a ghost would be heard on the hill."

It is said that the prince regent Duo'ergun in the early Qing Dynasty lived together with Empress Dowager Xiaozhuang, mother of Emperor Shunzhi (1644-1661), like man and wife.

Was Emperor Shunzhi's beloved Imperial Concubine Dong E beautiful? Was she really the famous prostitute Dong Xiaowan from the south?

According to someone's research, Baoyu, the hero of *A Dream of Red Mansions*, was modeled on the crown prince of Emperor Kangxi (reigned 1662-1722).

Was Emperor Yongzheng (reigned 1723-1735) really assassinated by a woman called Lü Siniang?

Was Emperor Guangxu (reigned 1875-1908) really killed by Empress Dowager Cixi? Who threw his favorite Imperial Concubine Zhen into the well? What did she see at that moment? Did she call to her beloved emperor?

There are many more questions....

How many stories have been spawned and how many secrets have been hidden in this sprawling palace complex that has existed for nearly 600 years?

We have no idea.

Maybe the birds that flew over it or the insects that once crawled around it knew. Maybe the crows that have lived there for generations know. Maybe the "fox fairies" in the deserted halls know. Maybe the ghosts of wronged people floating in the dark know. Maybe the Heavenly Emperor in the Purple Forbidden Enclosure knows.

But we don't know.

Let us ignore the confusing records and emerge from the labyrinth of documents. Let the Forbidden City fade into colorful lights and shadows. Carve it into an aesthetic image, and keep a beautiful memory of it in our heart. You can frame and color it as you will. You can narrate a history with dreamlike colors. You can interpret an impression with classical patterns. You can also create a Forbidden City of your own within your tender heart.

So nothing about it is distant anymore. When we integrate ourselves into the magnetite as small elements, we'll see ourselves in the stories.

We'll witness and experience the stories....

The emperor's home is so large, that I'm like a small ant in it. It was home to 24 emperors of the Ming and Qing dynasties.

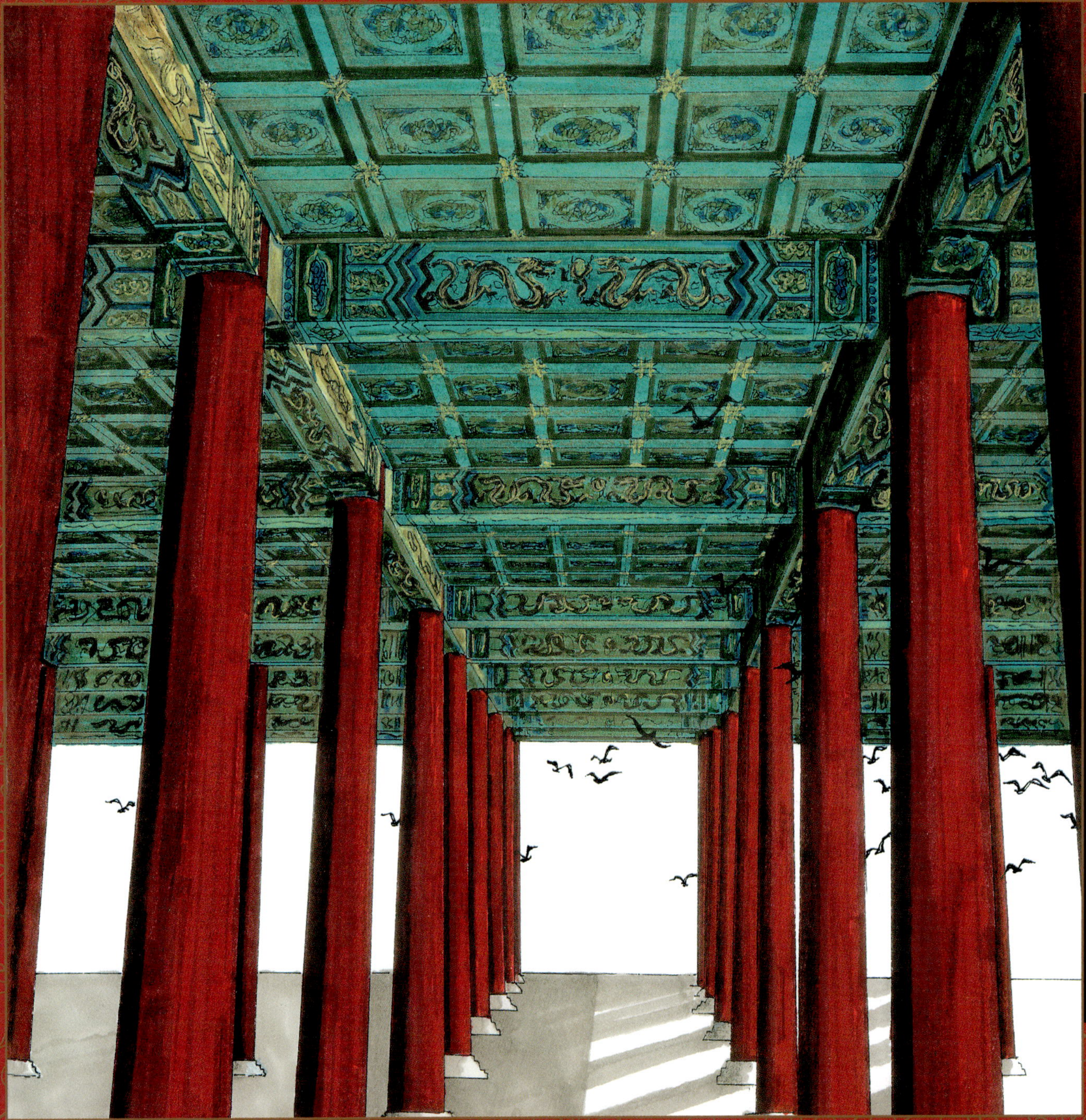

What is the meaning of "fair and square"? It shows the benevolence of the ways of Heaven and Earth. It is believed to be the characteristic virtue of the Heavenly Emperor.

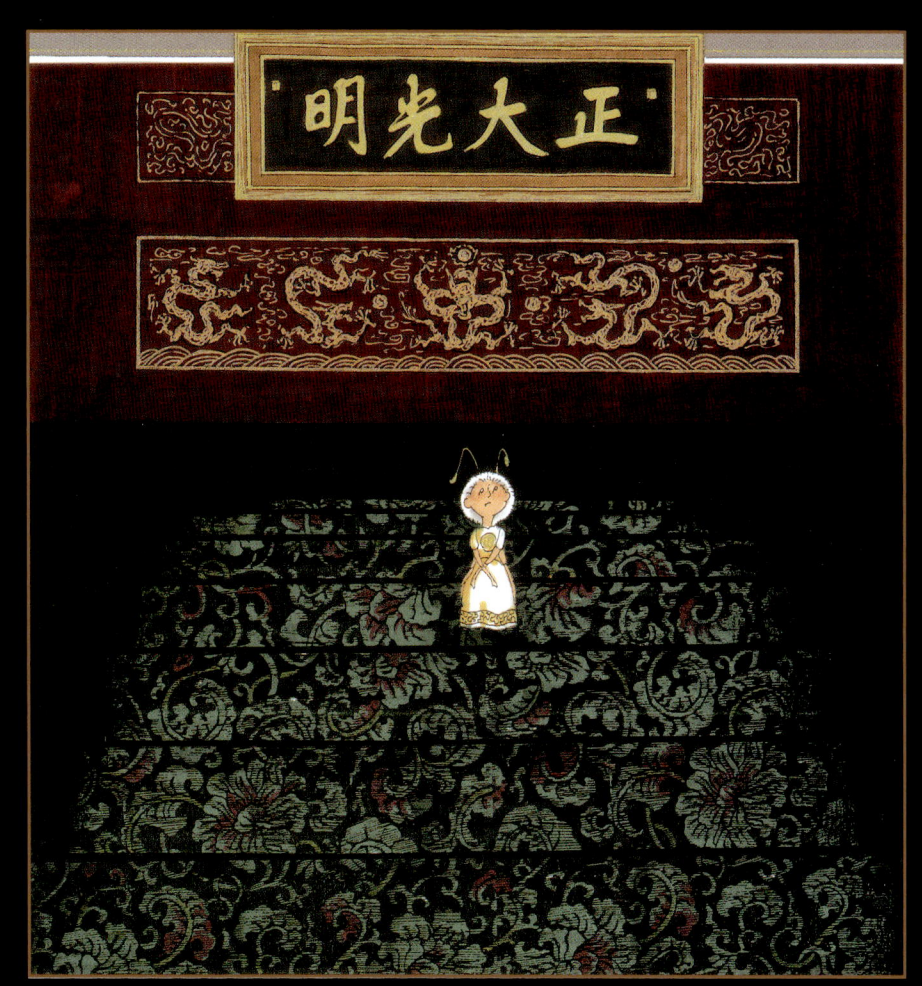

◁ The swallows and sparrows flying over the Forbidden City, untamed, were the most lively, free souls the large imperial palace saw.

▷ The gilded bronze halls flanking the base of the Palace of Heavenly Purity are called the Golden Halls of State Power. They represent the idea that "under the vault of Heaven, there is no place that is not the emperor's; on the shores that can be reached, there is no one who is not the emperor's subject."

How large is the Forbidden City? It is four times the size of the Louvre in France; nine times the size of the St. Petersburg Palace in Russia, and three times the size of the Imperial Palace in Tokyo. It is in fact the largest and most intact imperial palace extant in the world.

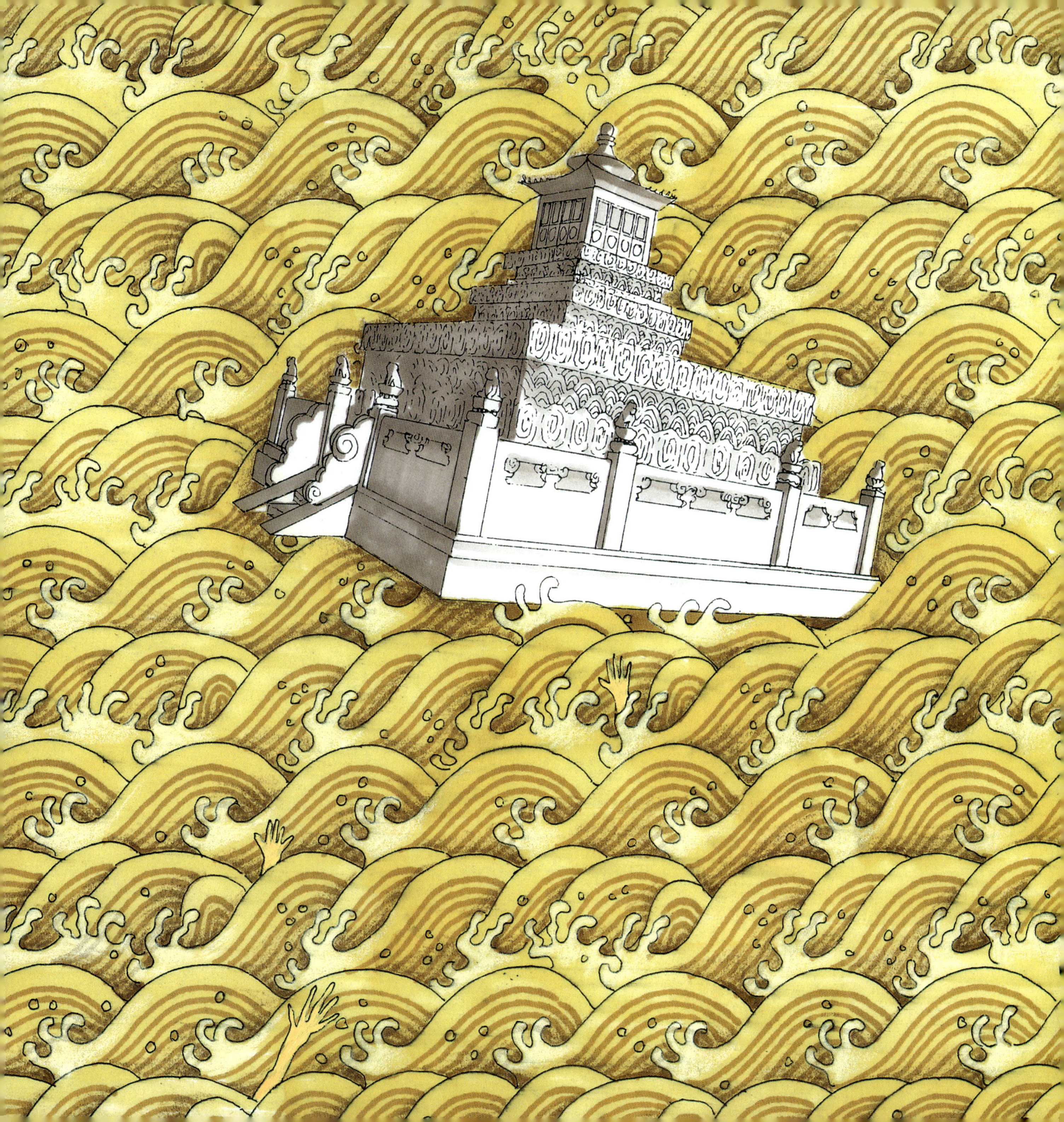

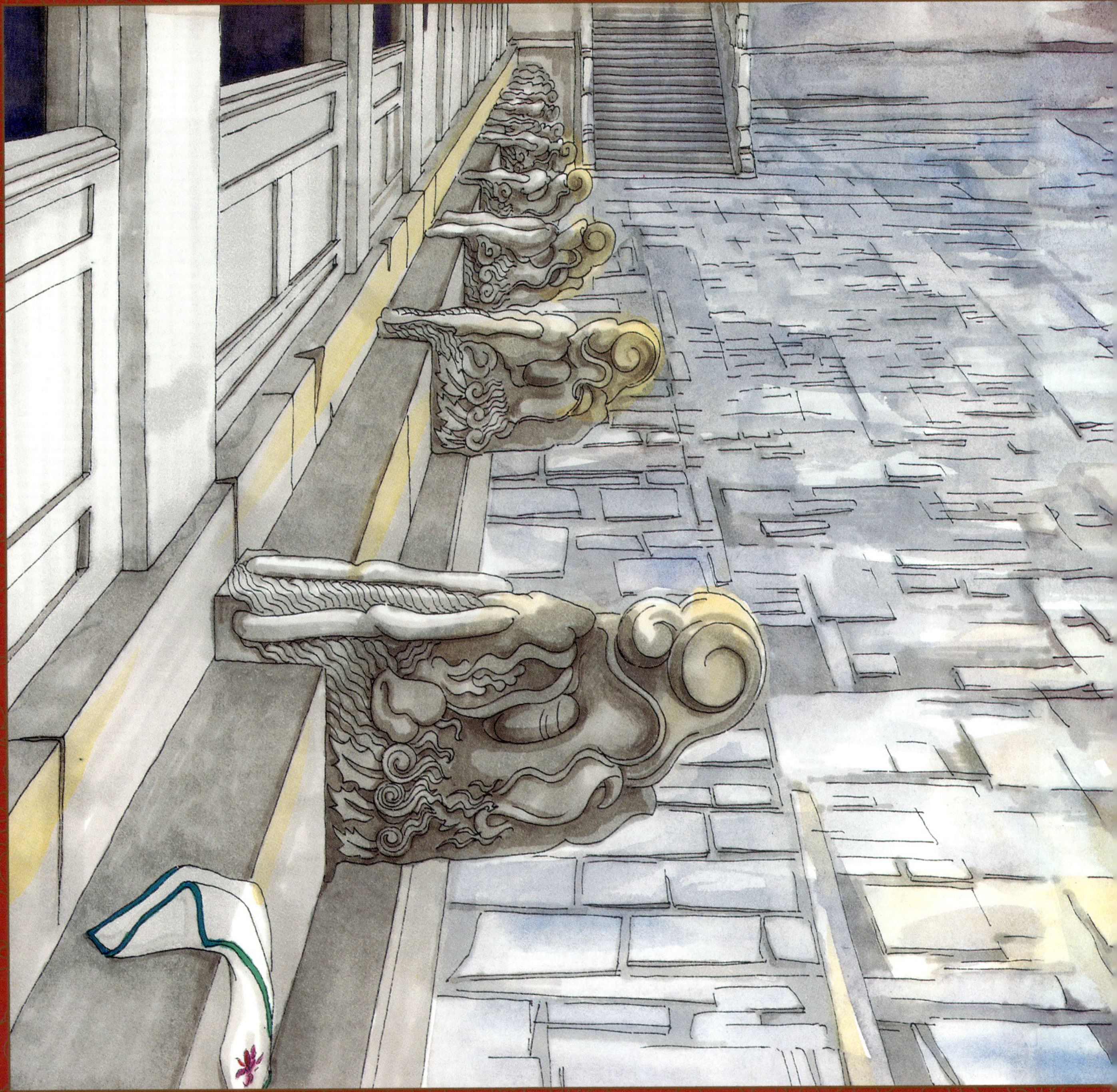

Has anyone seen the 1,142 hornless dragon heads discharging rainwater at the same time? It must be a magnificent sight.

The complicated slanting wooden clusters between the eaves and the beam are called brackets, and are said to have been structured according to the lever and scale principles. One feels dazed just looking at them.

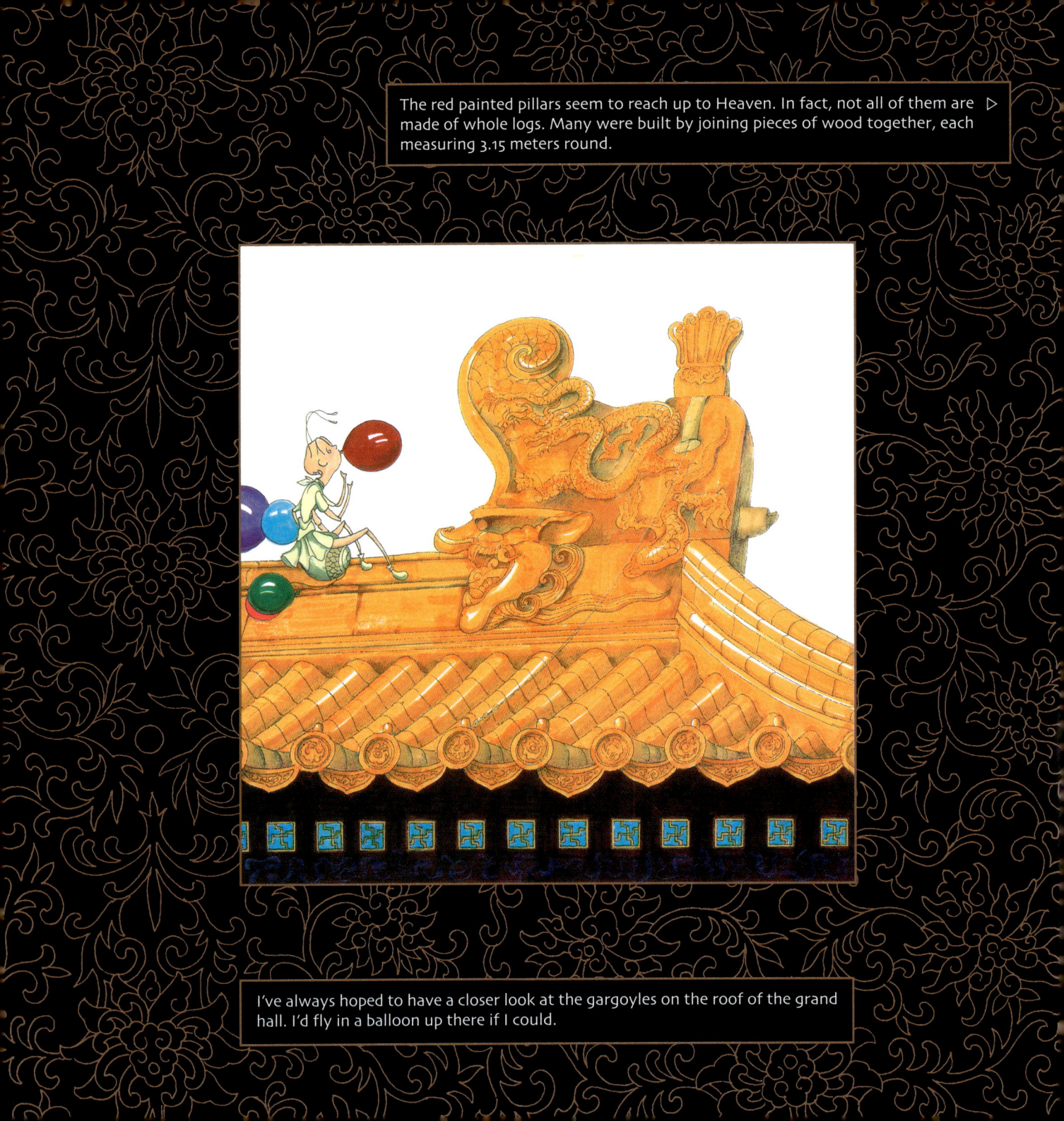

The red painted pillars seem to reach up to Heaven. In fact, not all of them are made of whole logs. Many were built by joining pieces of wood together, each measuring 3.15 meters round.

I've always hoped to have a closer look at the gargoyles on the roof of the grand hall. I'd fly in a balloon up there if I could.

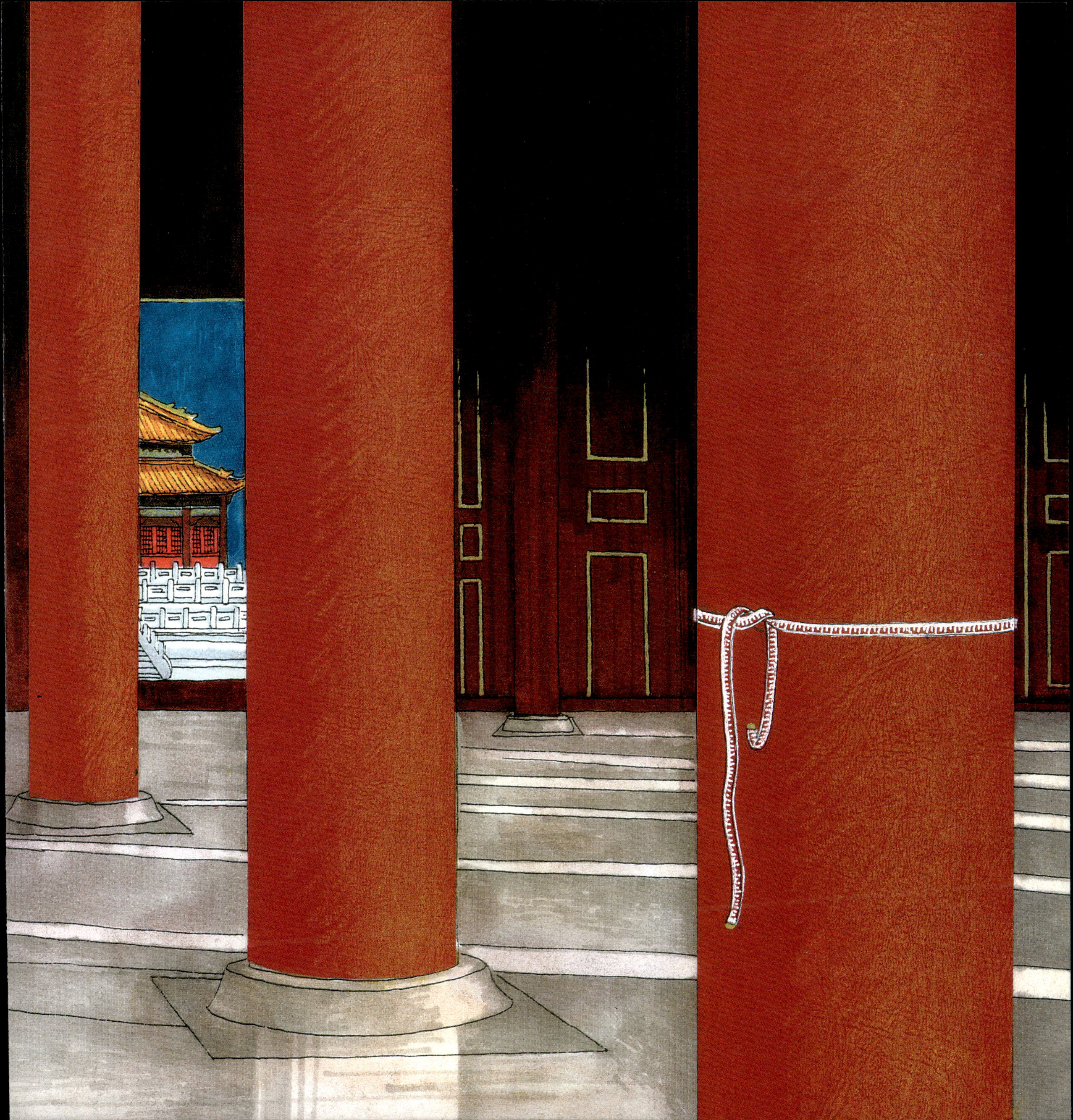

Why are you driving us away? Isn't it our home? Look at the patterns on the wall; they clearly originated with us.

A gate may separate us from another time and space. This gate of the Forbidden City symbolized the border line between Heaven and the world of man. There are 81 round-headed decorative nails in the gate, in nine horizontal and nine vertical rows. The number "nine" is a symbol of supremacy in Chinese tradition.

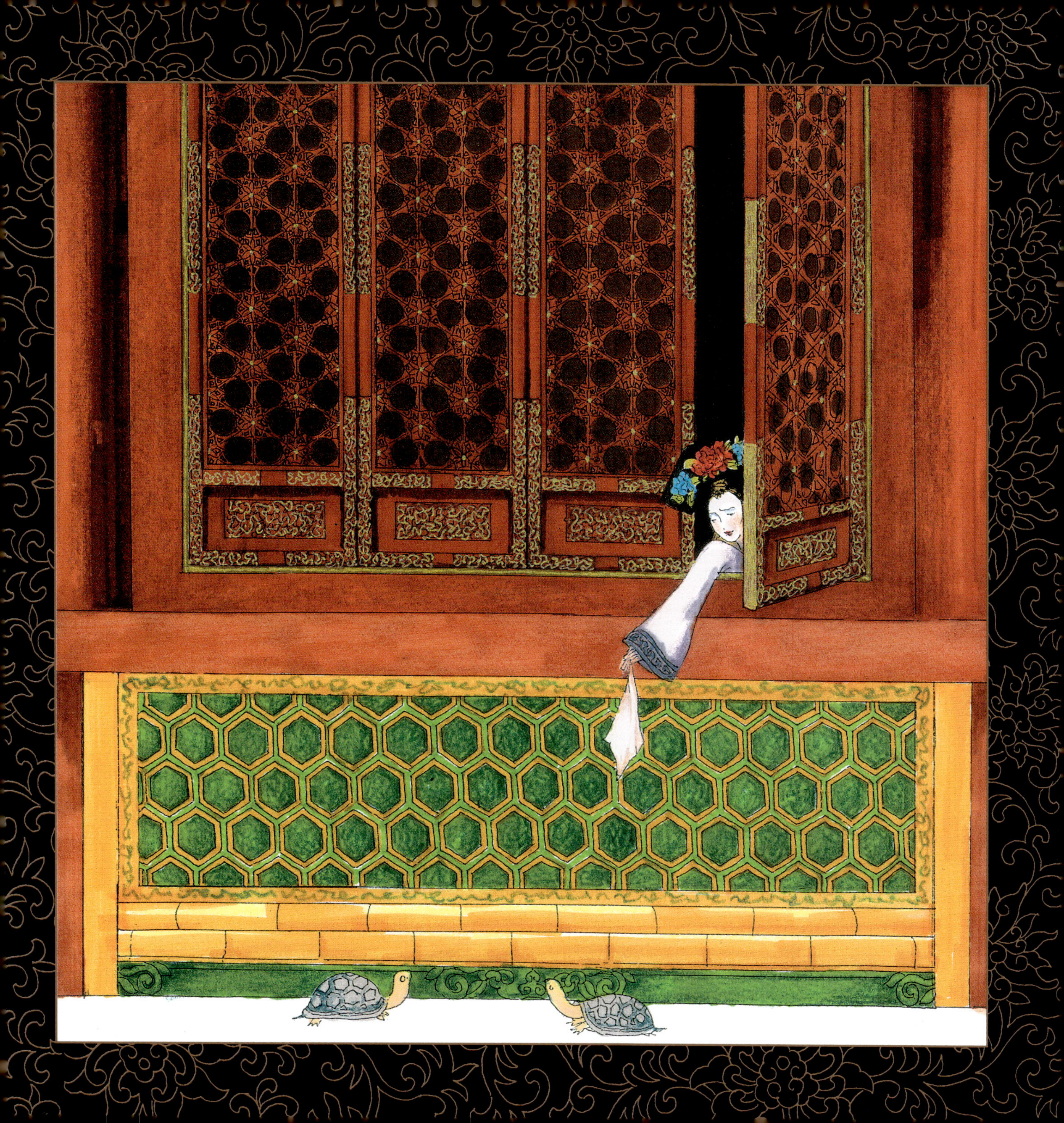

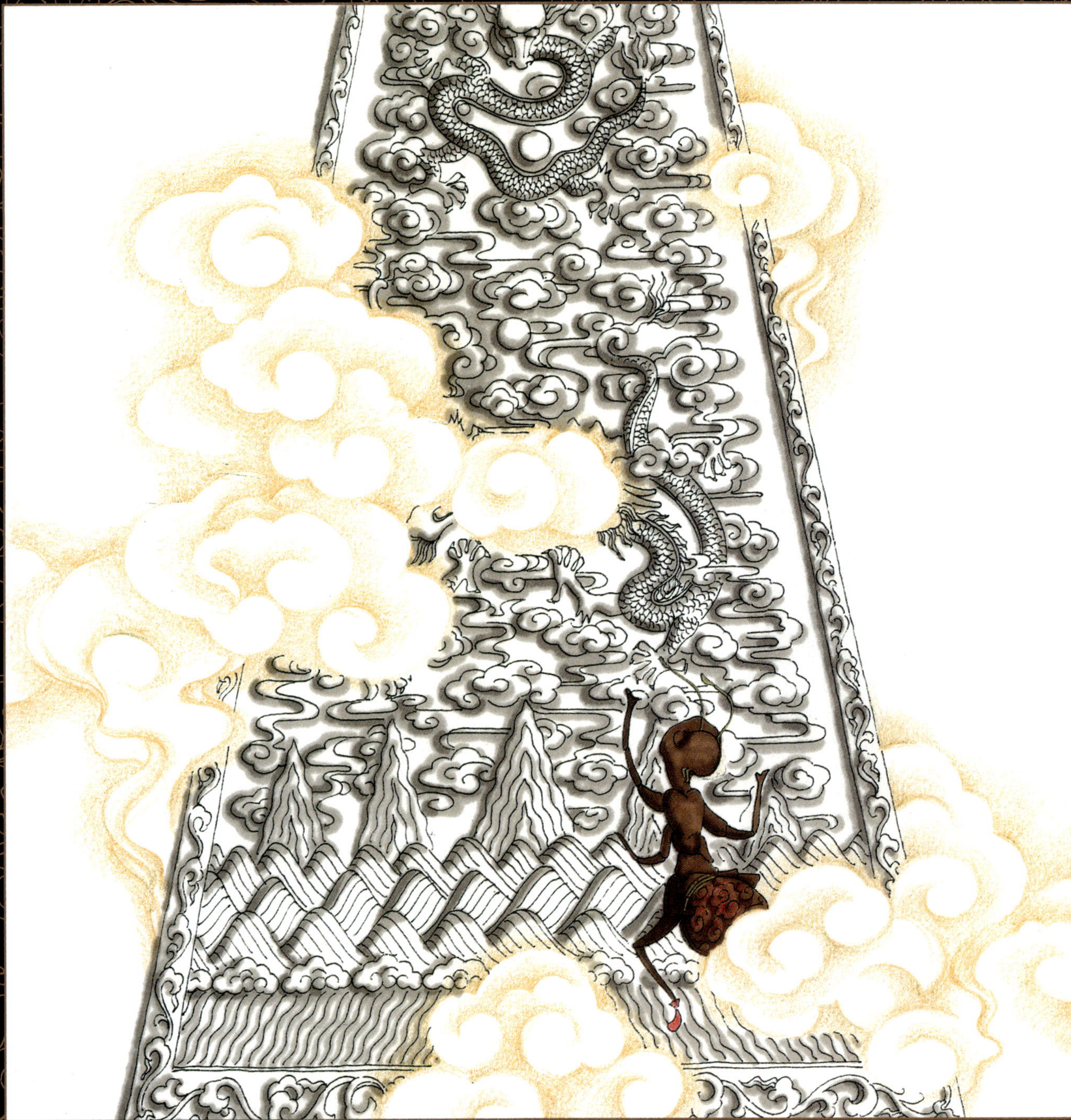

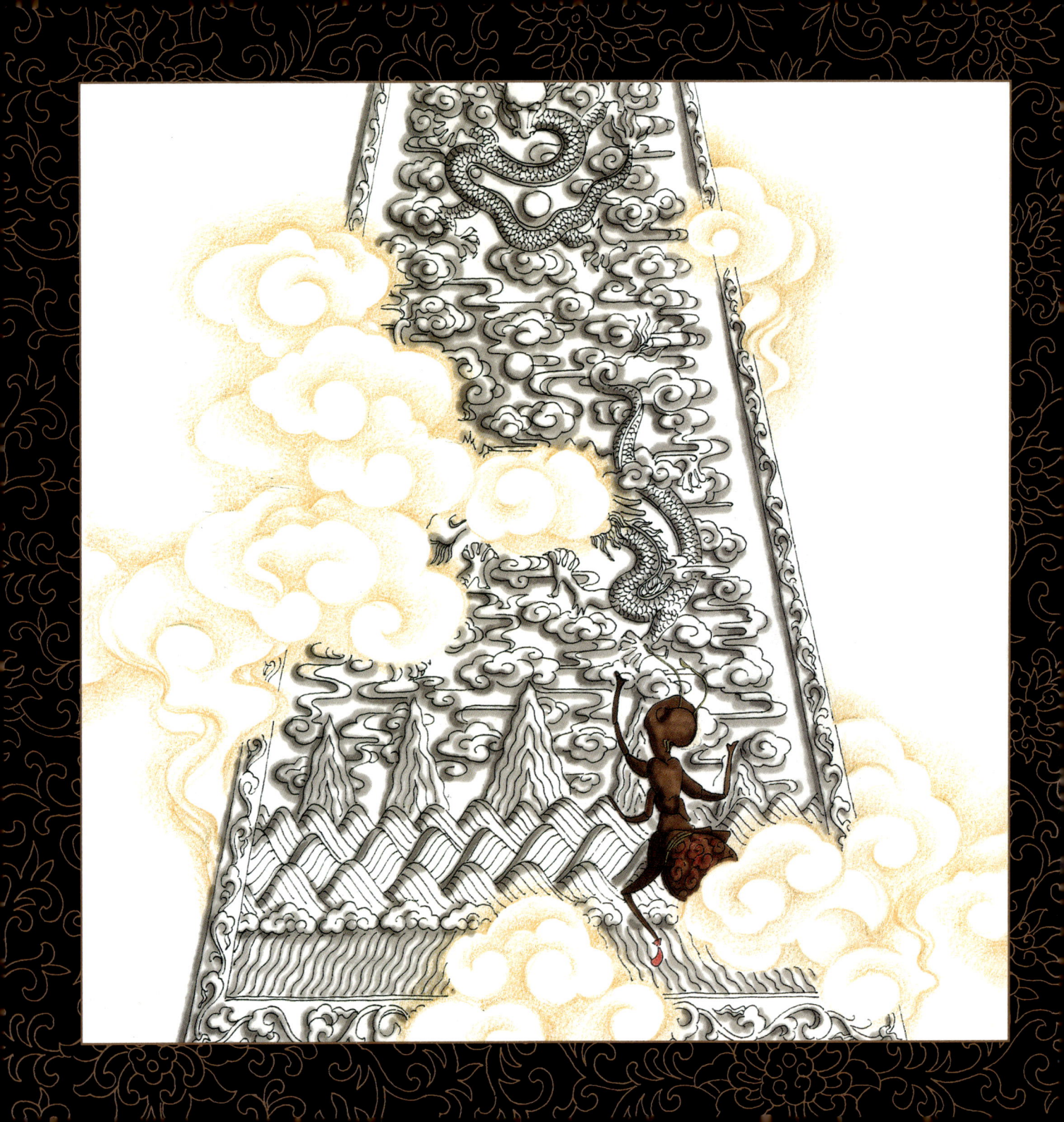

◁ It is impossible to climb up to Heaven from here.
But don't you know that you're in Heaven already?

The Forbidden City was named after the Purple Forbidden Enclosure in Heaven.

The jade plate of this sundial is evenly divided by 24 lines indicating the hours. The shadow of the needle moves with the sun. This ingenious device may be the earliest clock ever.

Many people don't know what ▷ this was for. It was a lamp post holder in the imperial palace during the Ming and Qing dynasties. It witnessed the grand lamp lighting ceremonies: "In the sleepless city, where the lamplight and moonlight blend, the emperor's entertainment lasts day and night."

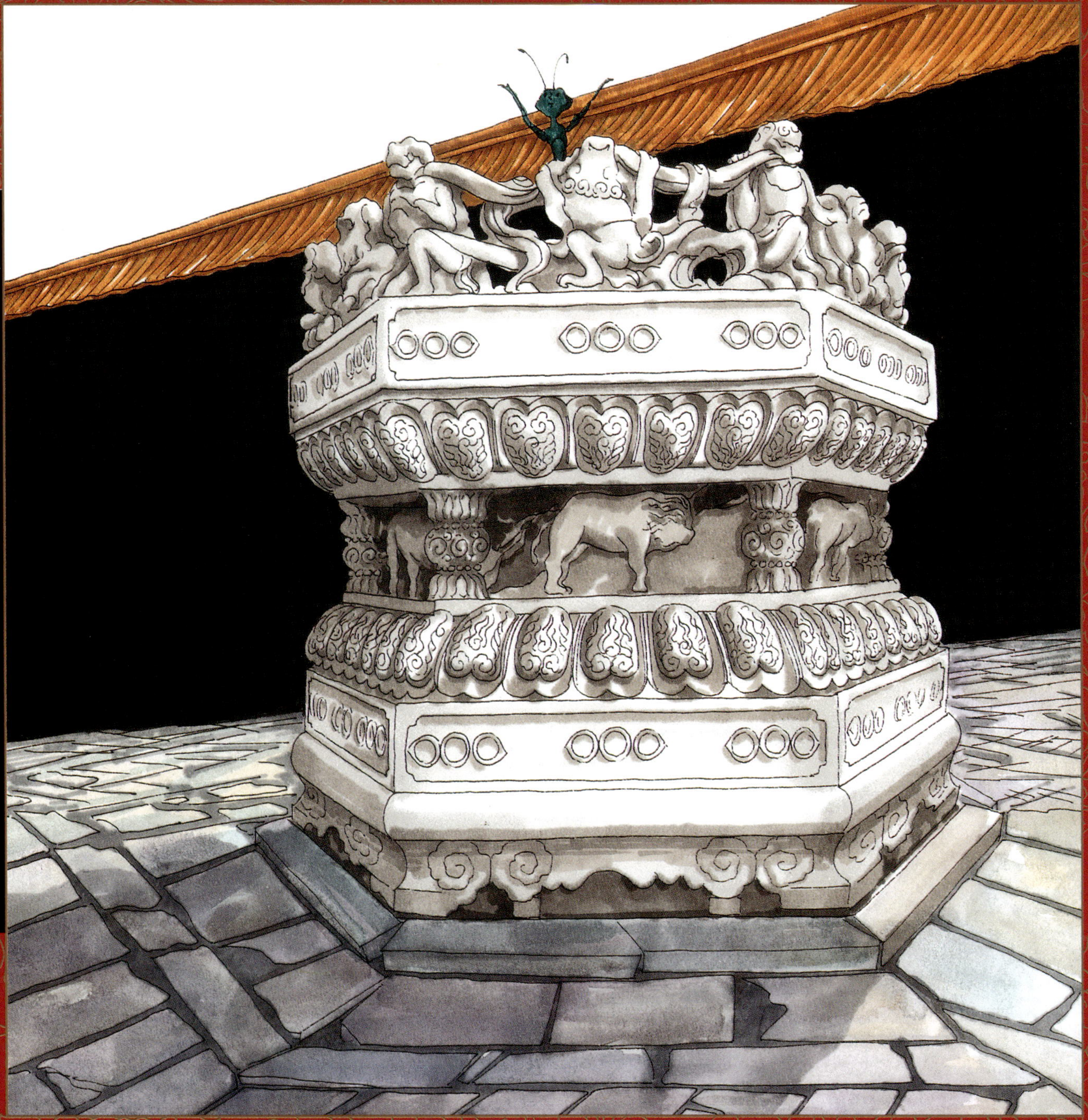

I love every corner here. It is a beautiful picture. The ornaments on the walls, tiles on the roofs, and floral patterns along the paths are all too exquisite to miss.

It is said that there are 9,999.5 rooms in the Forbidden City, because there are 10,000 rooms in the palace of the Jade Emperor in Heaven. So the emperor, believing himself to be the "Son of Heaven," dared not have as many rooms in his own palace, so he had half a room less. As a matter of fact, there are 8,707 rooms.

I call this work "Air-tight Heaven." I didn't paint it though. I wonder how my teacher would rate the work of our ancestors.

Is this crane aspiring to "return home riding on the wind?" If so, why has it been standing here for 500 years? Is its aspiration really our wish too?

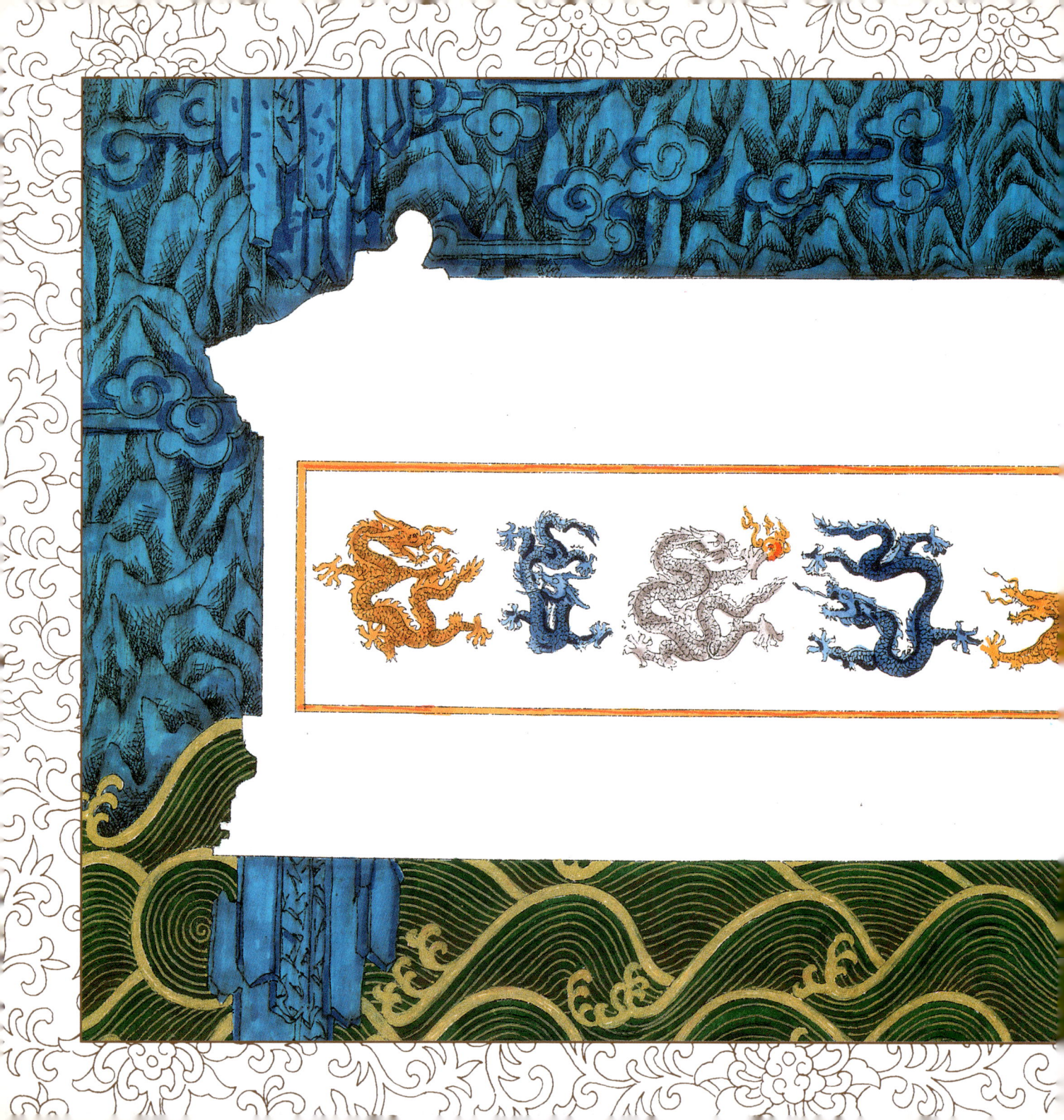

This Nine Dragon Wall has more than 18 dragons on both sides. Look carefully, and you'll be surprised to find that there are 635 large and small dragons.

The layout of the Forbidden City is symmetrical. There are left and right wing gates, middle left and right gates, and so on. See this West Long Lane? Come with me to see East Long Lane.

The palace is as divinely beautiful as a paradise, and neither "splendid city in Heaven" nor "abode of immortals in the sea" are enough to describe its beauty.

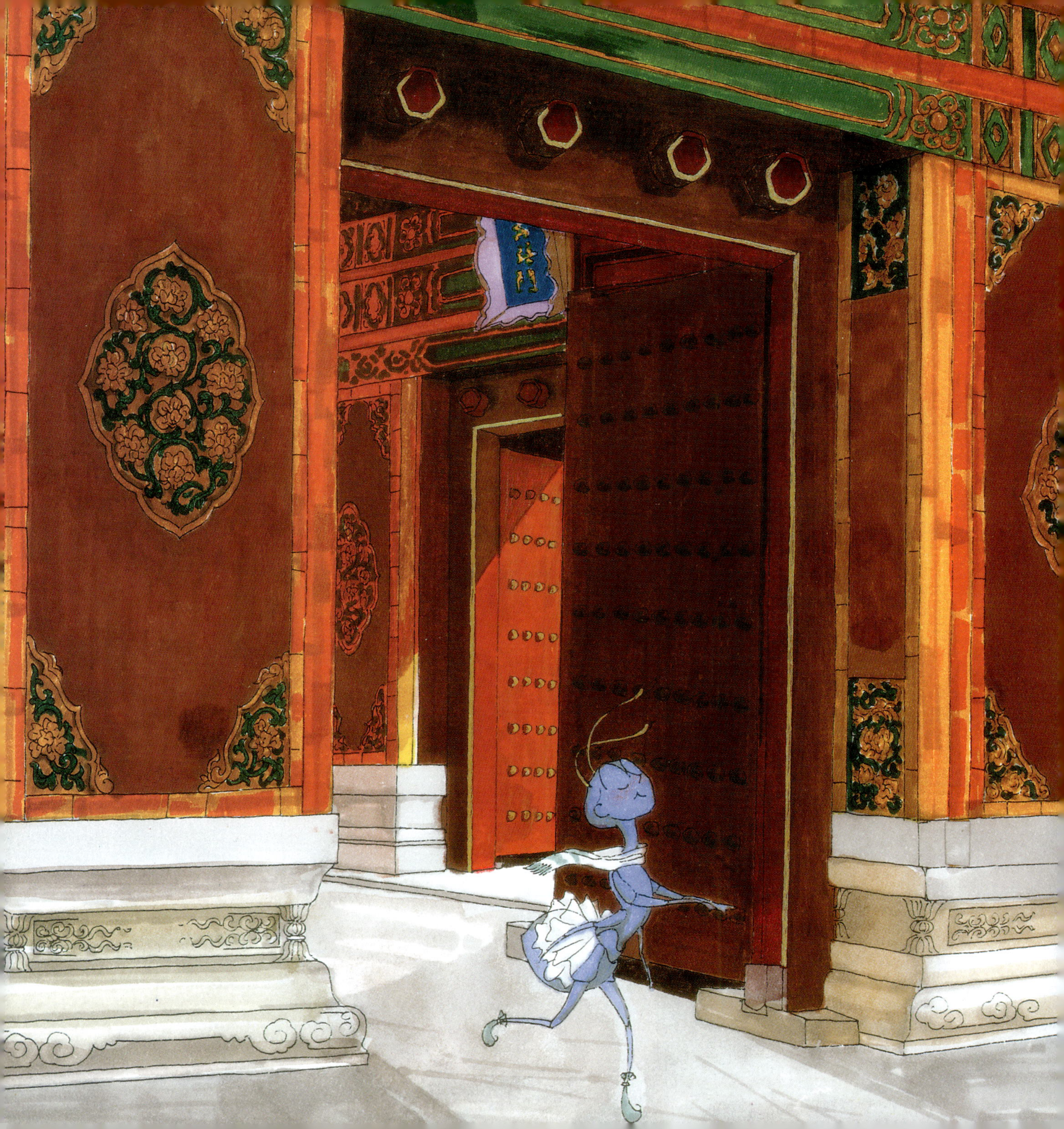

◁ The Forbidden City is a mysterious place. When you enter it, you have to think like a historian and gaze like an artist....

Do you hear the deep, furious roaring of the lions? It seems to be of the same tempo as that of the Yellow River. But they are restrained and suppressed in the palace.

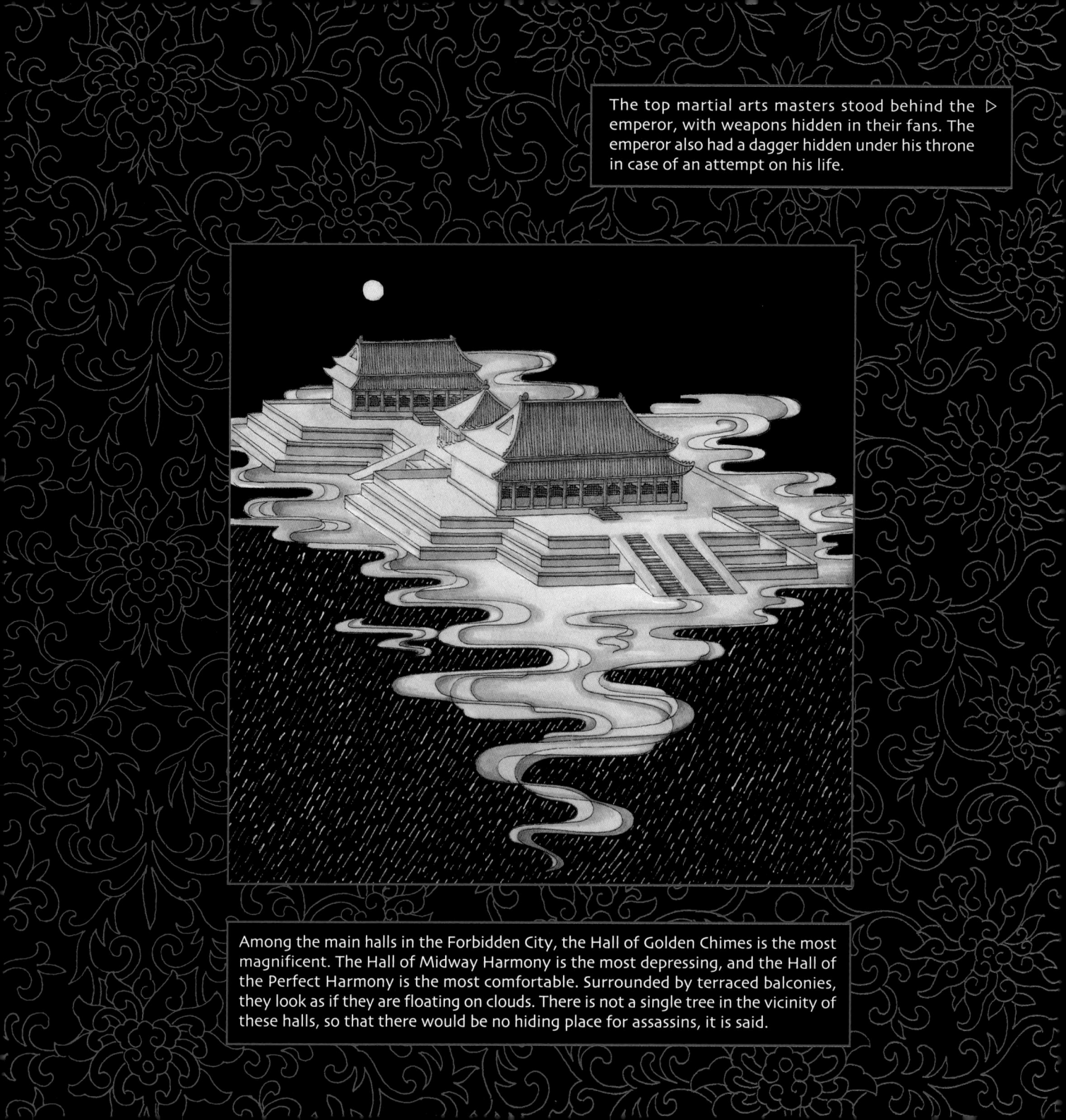

The top martial arts masters stood behind the ▷ emperor, with weapons hidden in their fans. The emperor also had a dagger hidden under his throne in case of an attempt on his life.

Among the main halls in the Forbidden City, the Hall of Golden Chimes is the most magnificent. The Hall of Midway Harmony is the most depressing, and the Hall of the Perfect Harmony is the most comfortable. Surrounded by terraced balconies, they look as if they are floating on clouds. There is not a single tree in the vicinity of these halls, so that there would be no hiding place for assassins, it is said.

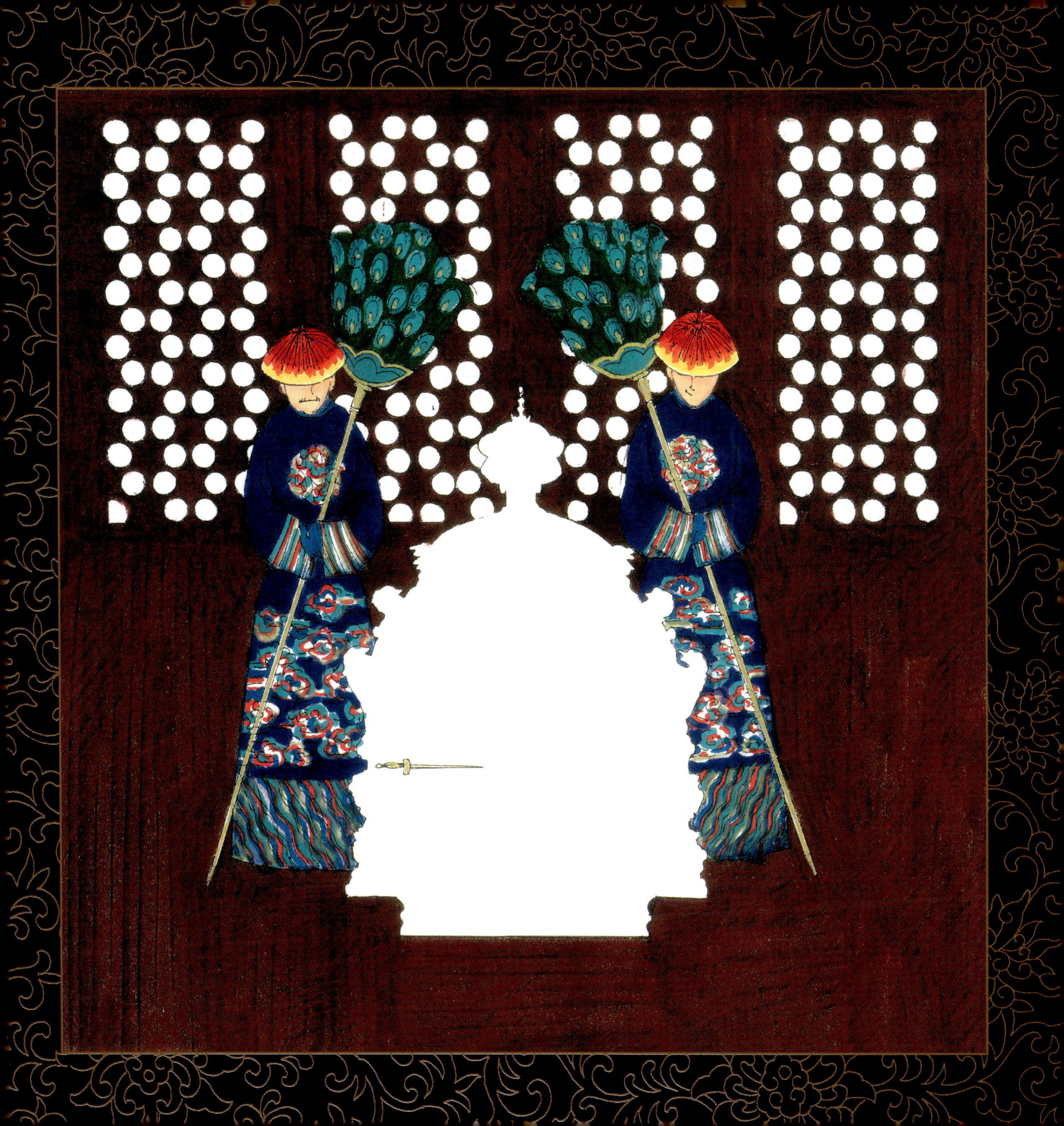

At noon, it is hard to find shade to escape from the scorching sun.

The ceremony of "offering captives" was traditionally held in front of the Meridian Gate. The Ming and Qing dynasties followed the tradition. In the Ming Dynasty, a special punishment called "court flogging" was meted out here. This place also served as an arsenal as well as something like a museum to display the merits of the founding emperors.

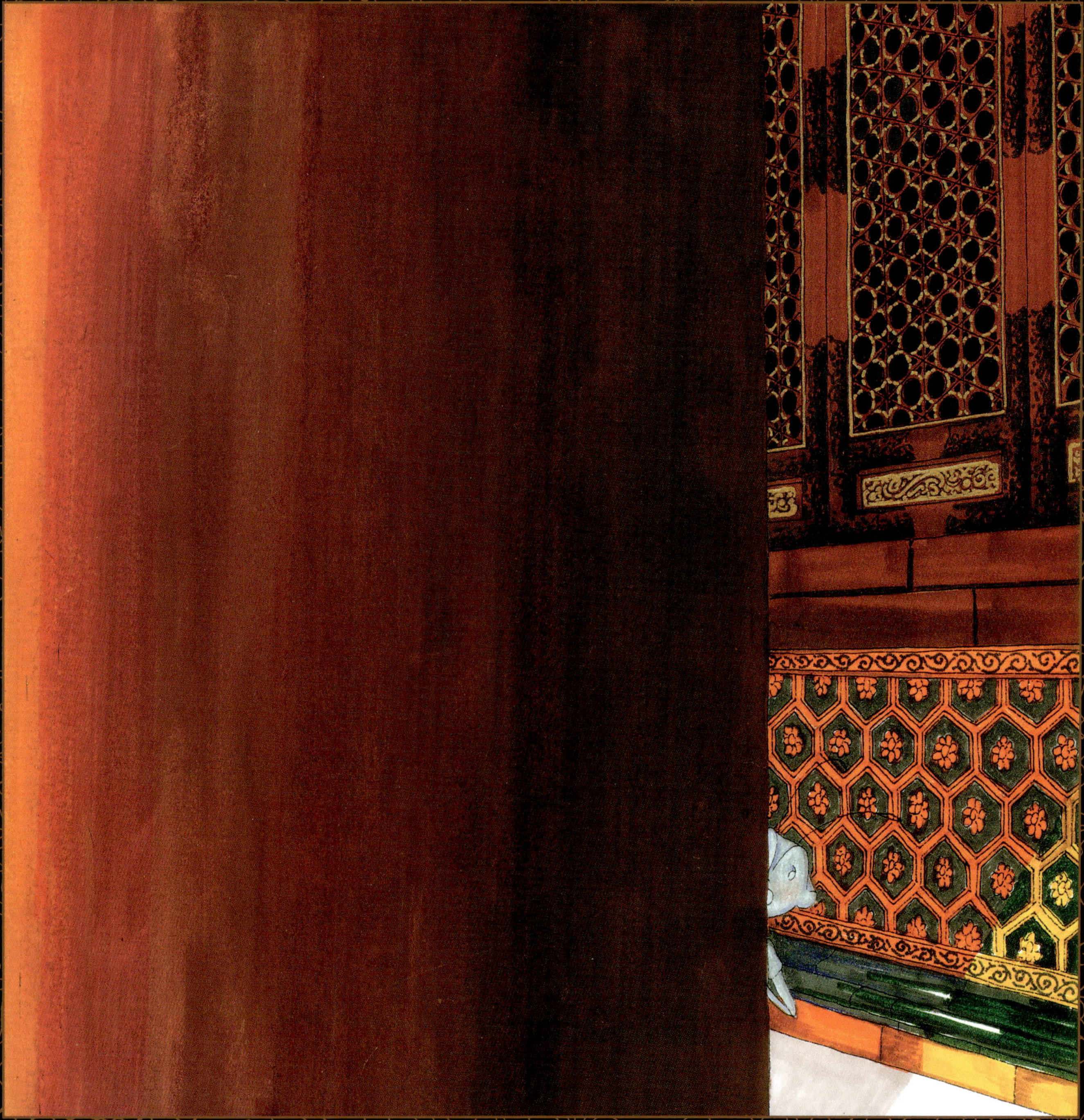

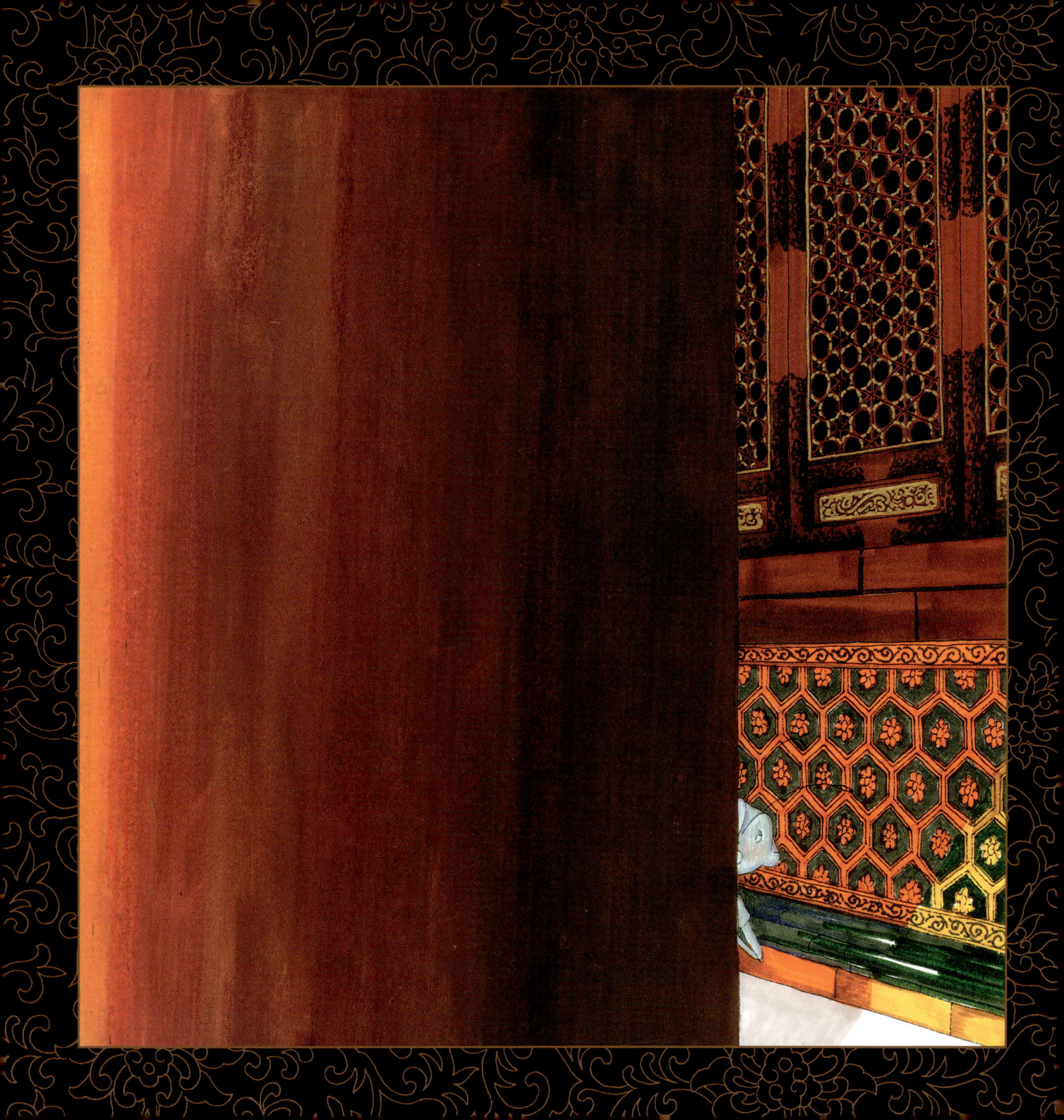

◁ The construction of this palace began when the Ming Dynasty Emperor Yongle ordered it to be built, in 1406. The main buildings were completed in 1420.

I can't see the whole of Heaven, but the blue color above my head provides me with enough space for imagination. Sometimes it rains, sometimes it snows, and sometimes it rains leaves.

Whenever I smell the fragrance, I forget where I am. ▷

With this beautiful pair of wings, I imagine myself flying into the heavenly palace.

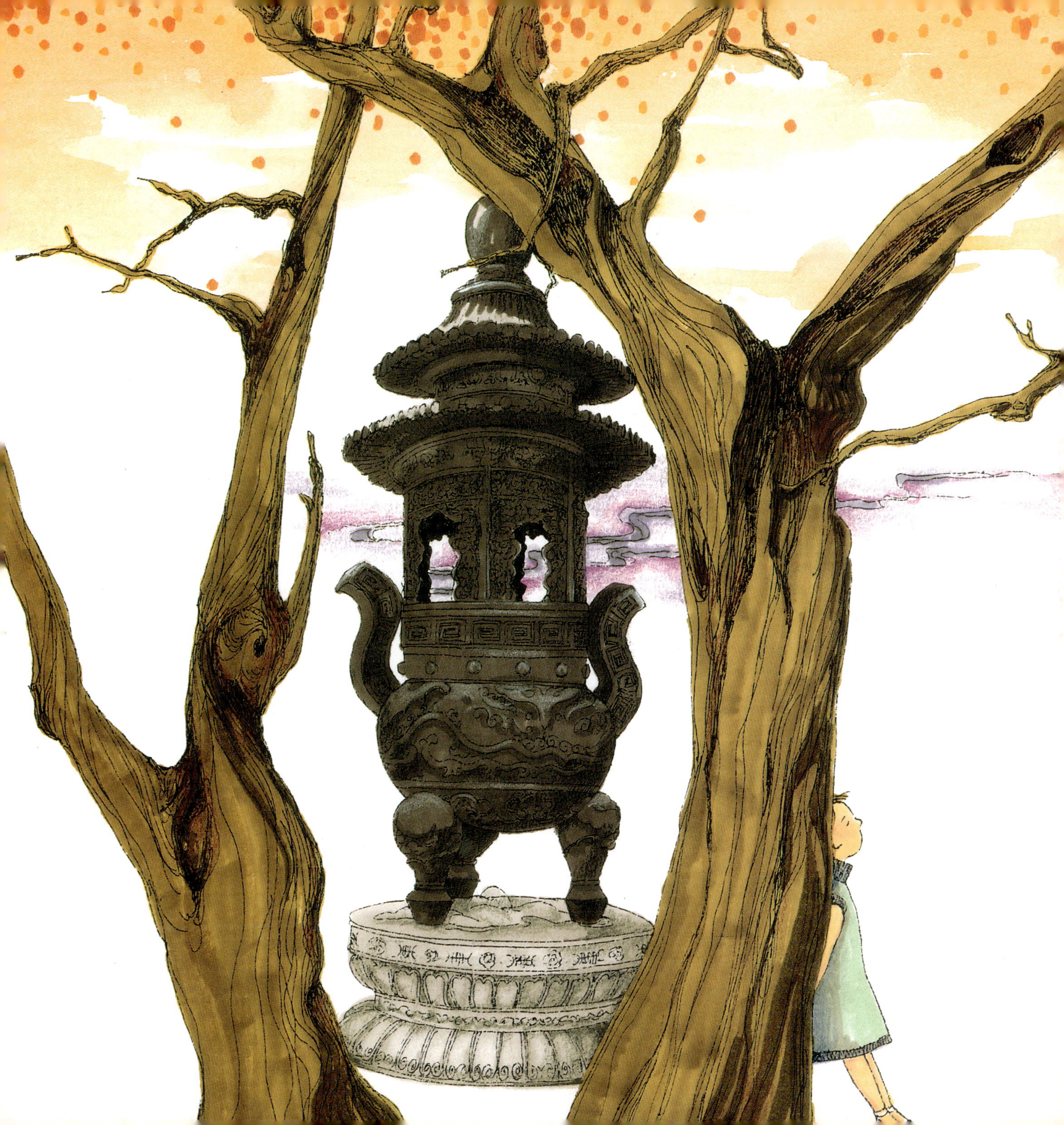

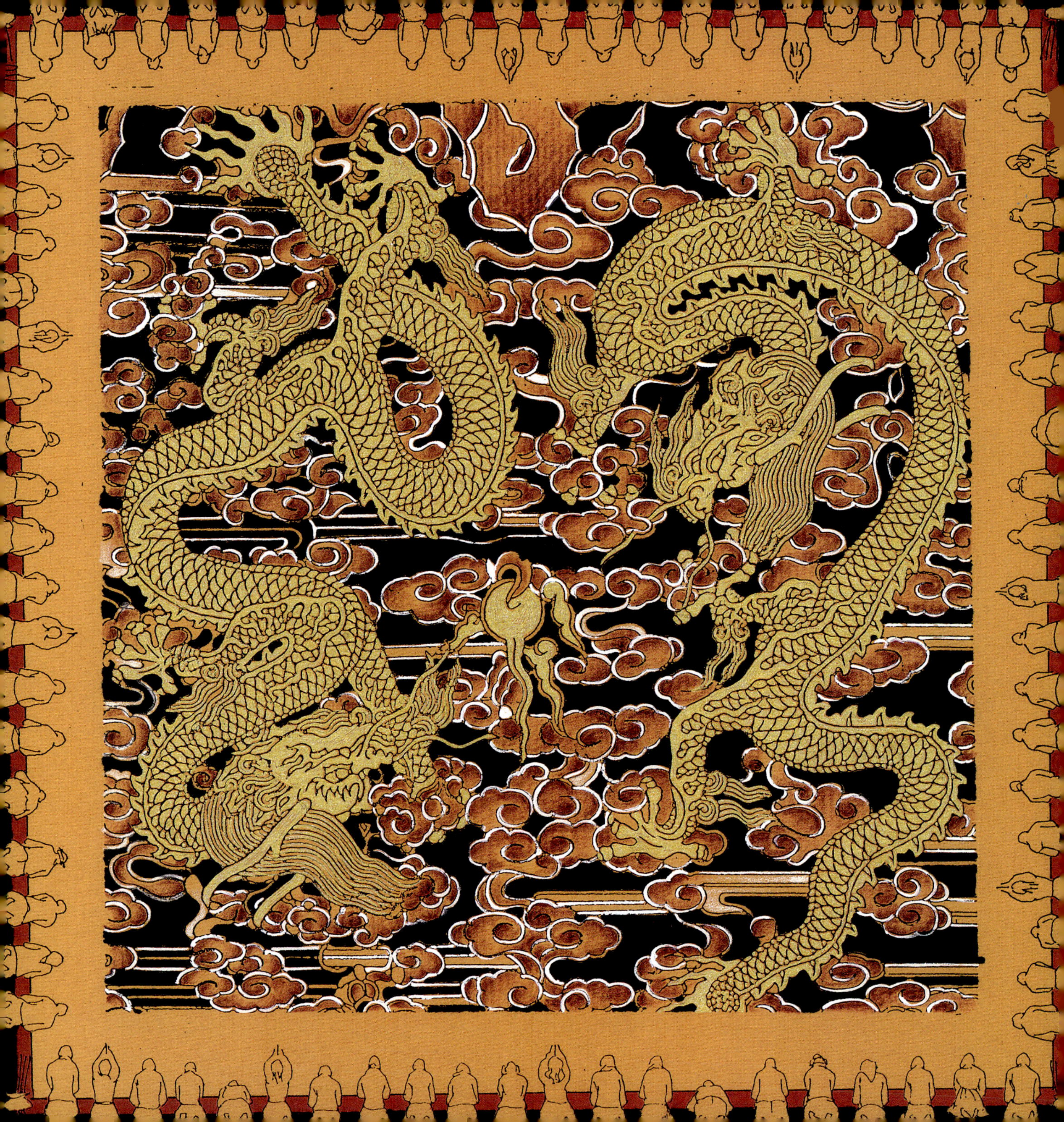

◁ The "dragon" dominates the Forbidden City. Every yellow-skinned Chinese is willing to be "bound" by this mysterious symbol and yield to its power wherever he or she goes, even today.

The "dragon throne" on which the emperor used to sit when handling state affairs was also called the "golden throne." It was the most exalted seat in the world.

There are all kinds of gates in the Forbidden City: house-shaped gates, memorial arch gates, floral-pendant gates.... This floral-pendant gate with a diadem-shaped top was exclusive to the emperor. Even princes were not allowed to pass through it.

The emperor lived in this room without any electric appliances. Perhaps he wouldn't have needed so many concubines if he'd had a TV set or video game player.

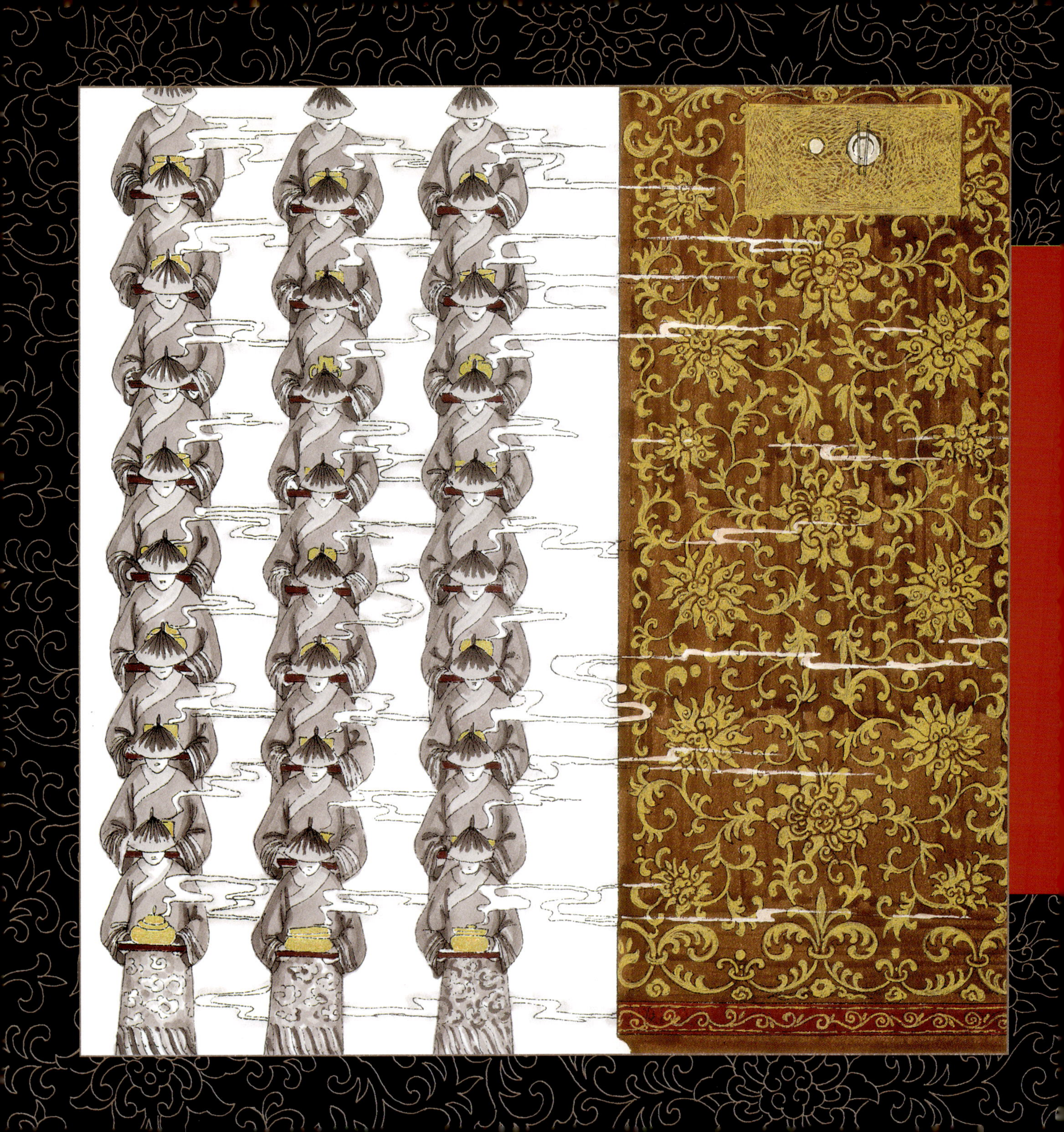

Hush, the emperor's sleeping!

◁ "The emperor's meal is ready," and the music starts. The emperor walks to the table surrounded by eunuchs. Actually the emperor didn't eat much. His leftovers were distributed to the concubines and ministers.

The emperor's health was not only the concern of the Imperial Academy of Medicine, but of every minister. It was critical to the state's power.

Do you know why many gates in the Forbidden City have no ▷ threshold? The last emperor ordered that the thresholds be removed so that he could ride his bicycle wherever he wanted.

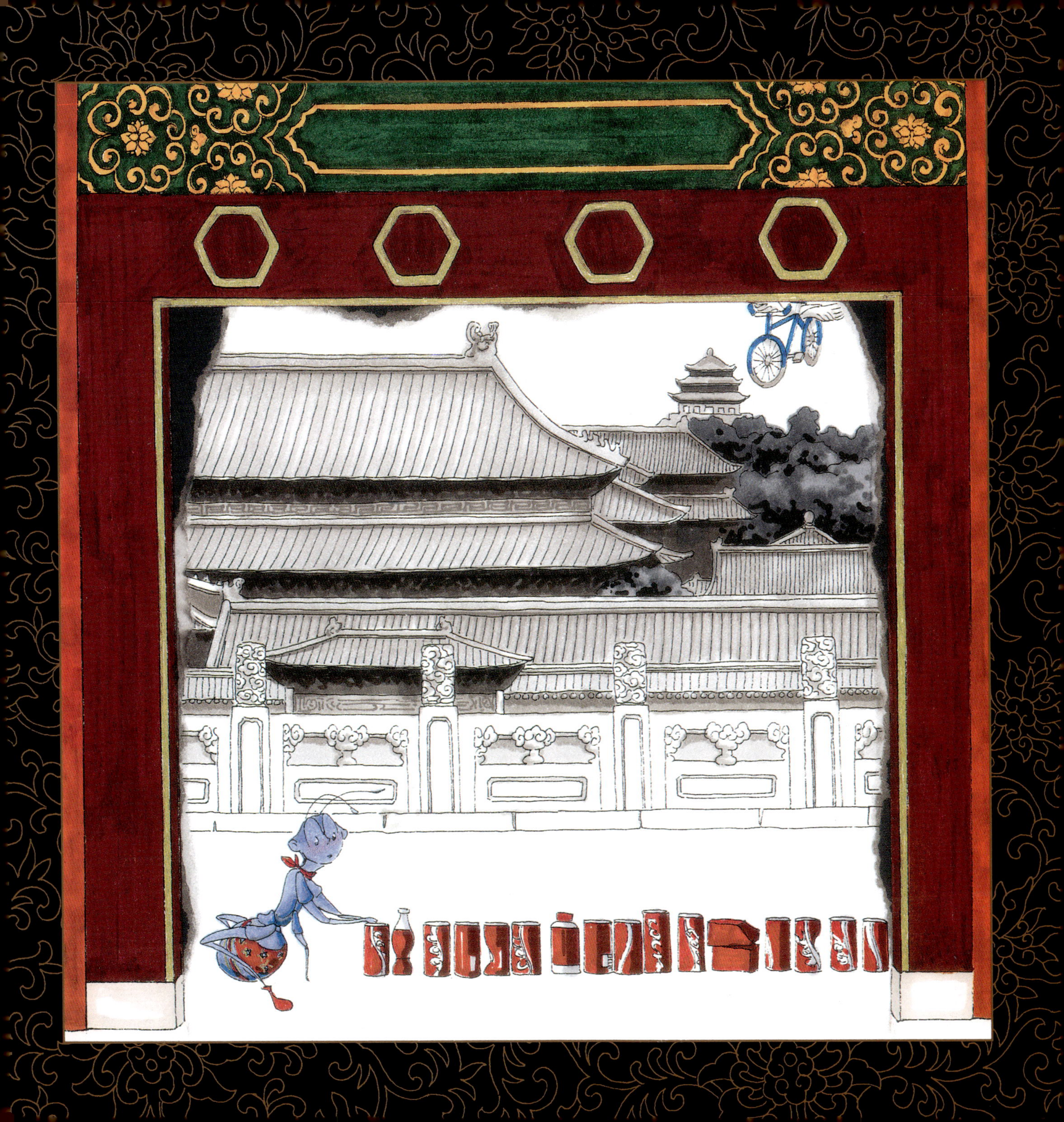

These rare objects were bribes sent to the emperor.

The place where the sons and grandsons of the emperor went to school was called the "Supreme Academy." It is located in the Palace of Heavenly Purity, close to where the emperor lived, so that he could inspect them at any time. The children went to school at the age of four or five, and left when they were given a title, a special residence and an official position. The green tiles on the roof indicate that it used to be a place frequented by sons and grandsons of the emperor.

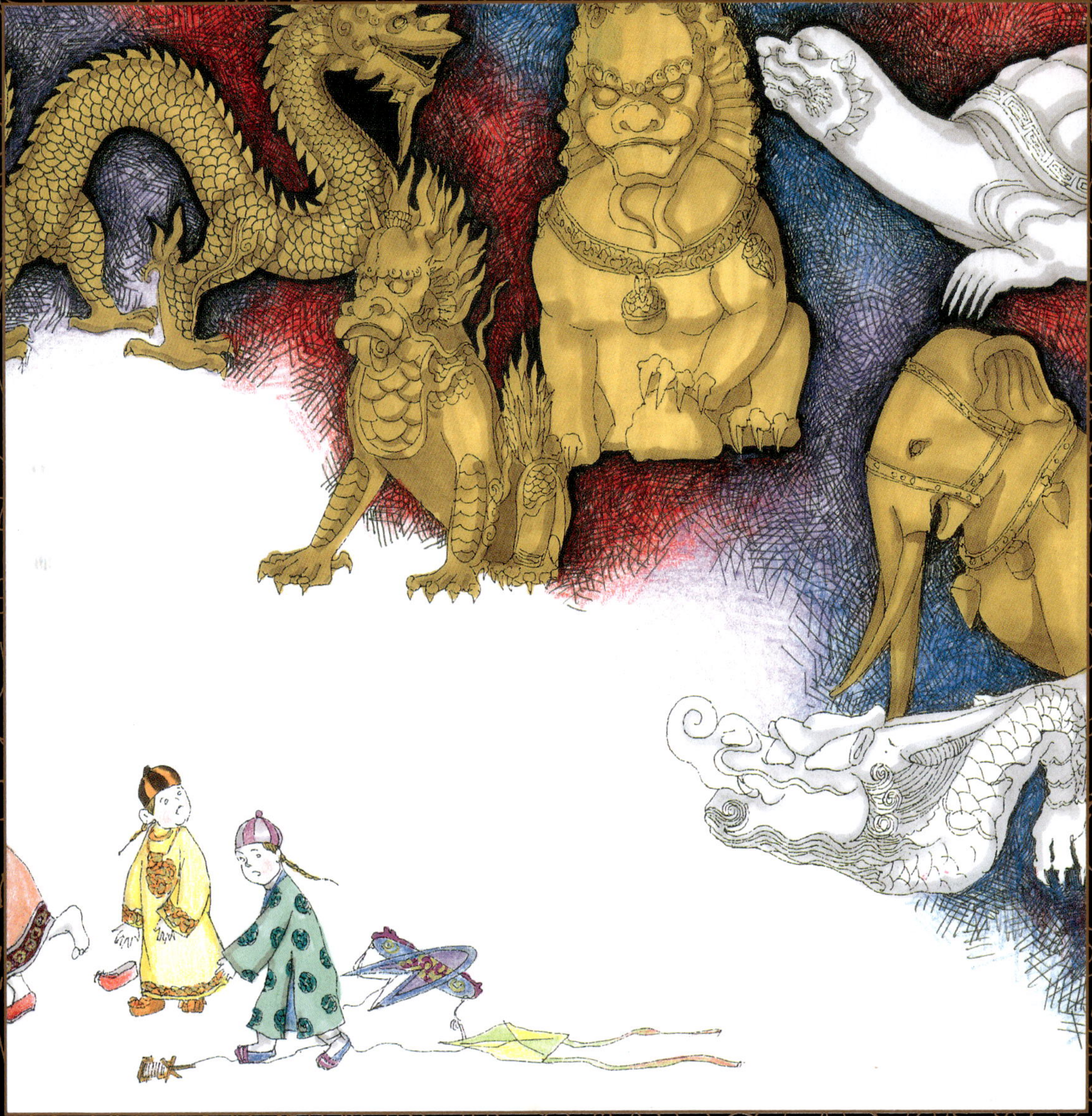

◁ I don't believe that the kids in the imperial palace led a life as happy as ours. Everything there was so sublime and mysterious that it struck them with awe.

Don't they say that there cannot be two suns in the sky?

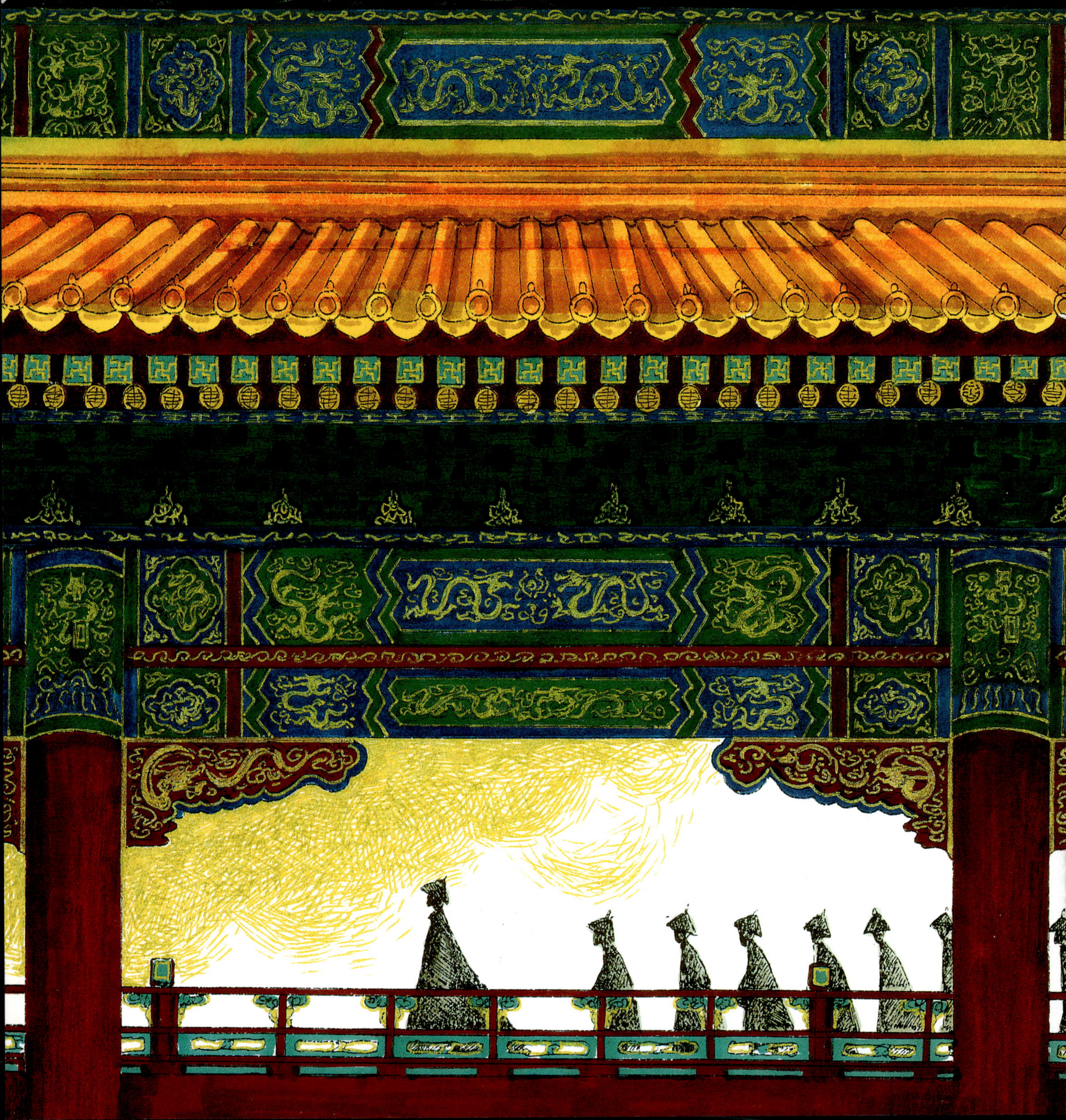

◁ The Forbidden City itself is like a large stage, with beautiful settings, bizarre stories and mysterious characters.

A eunuch, a miserable and sometimes detestable denizen of the palace.

Besides grandiosity there is rapidly spreading conspiracy..., ▷
for sunlight is blocked from this huge palace.

Eunuchs were in the emperor's favor during the Ming Dynasty. There were once 100,000 of them in the palace complex. During Emperor Qianlong's reign, there were 2,600 eunuchs there. The number was 2,000 when the eight-power allied forces invaded Beijing in 1900.

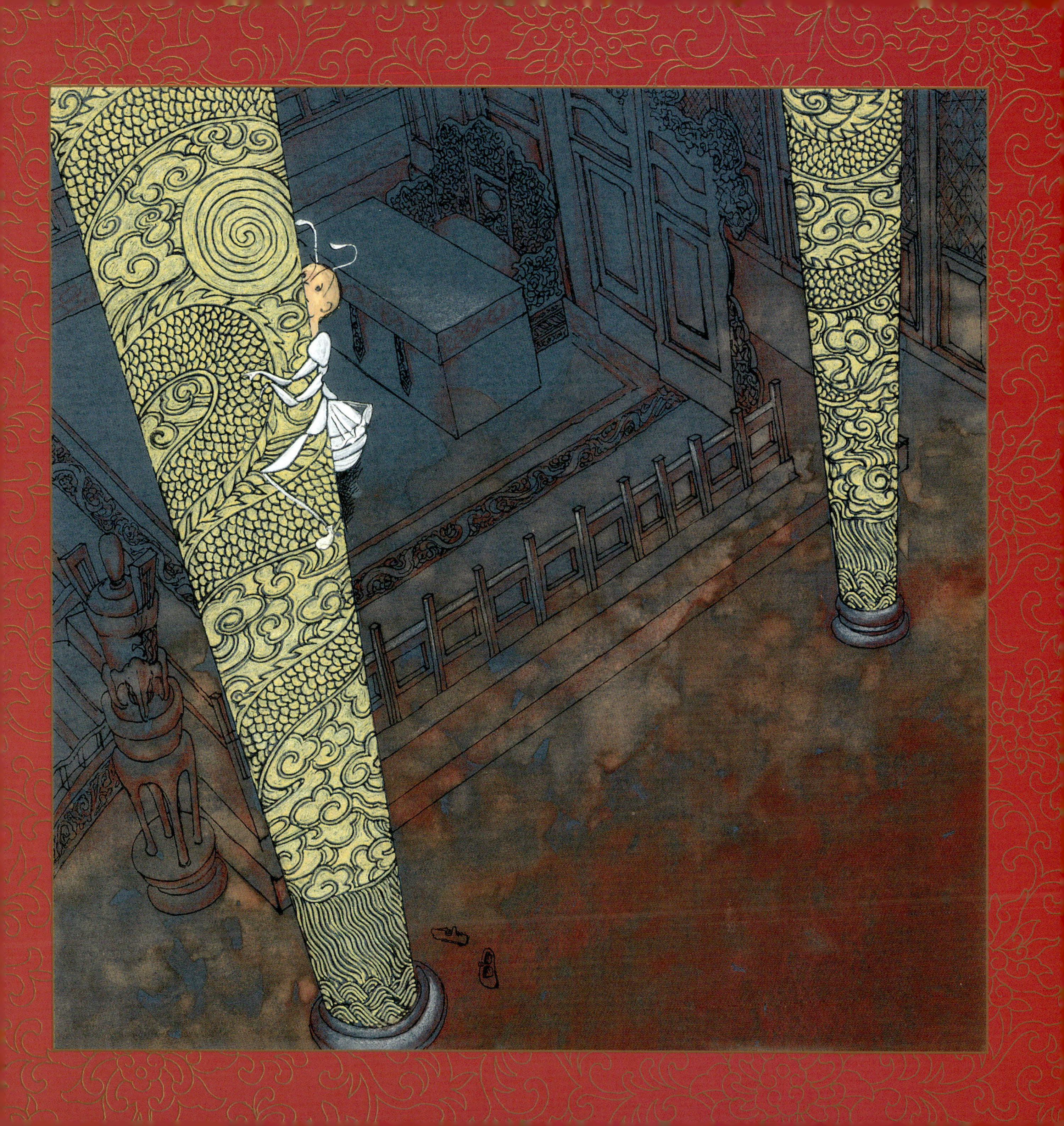

Have I ever had the power to reprimand someone else?

On his mother's 60th birthday, Emperor Qianlong built for her the Ten-Thousand-Buddha ▷ Tower with 10,000 niches inside. To fill the niches, he ordered that each of his officials in the capital and in the provinces should present him a gold statue of the Buddha. Then the common people had to pay tribute to the officials, who paid tribute to the emperor, who gave presents to his mother, who dedicated them to the Buddha. But the Buddha has nothing in his mind but the well-being of all things.

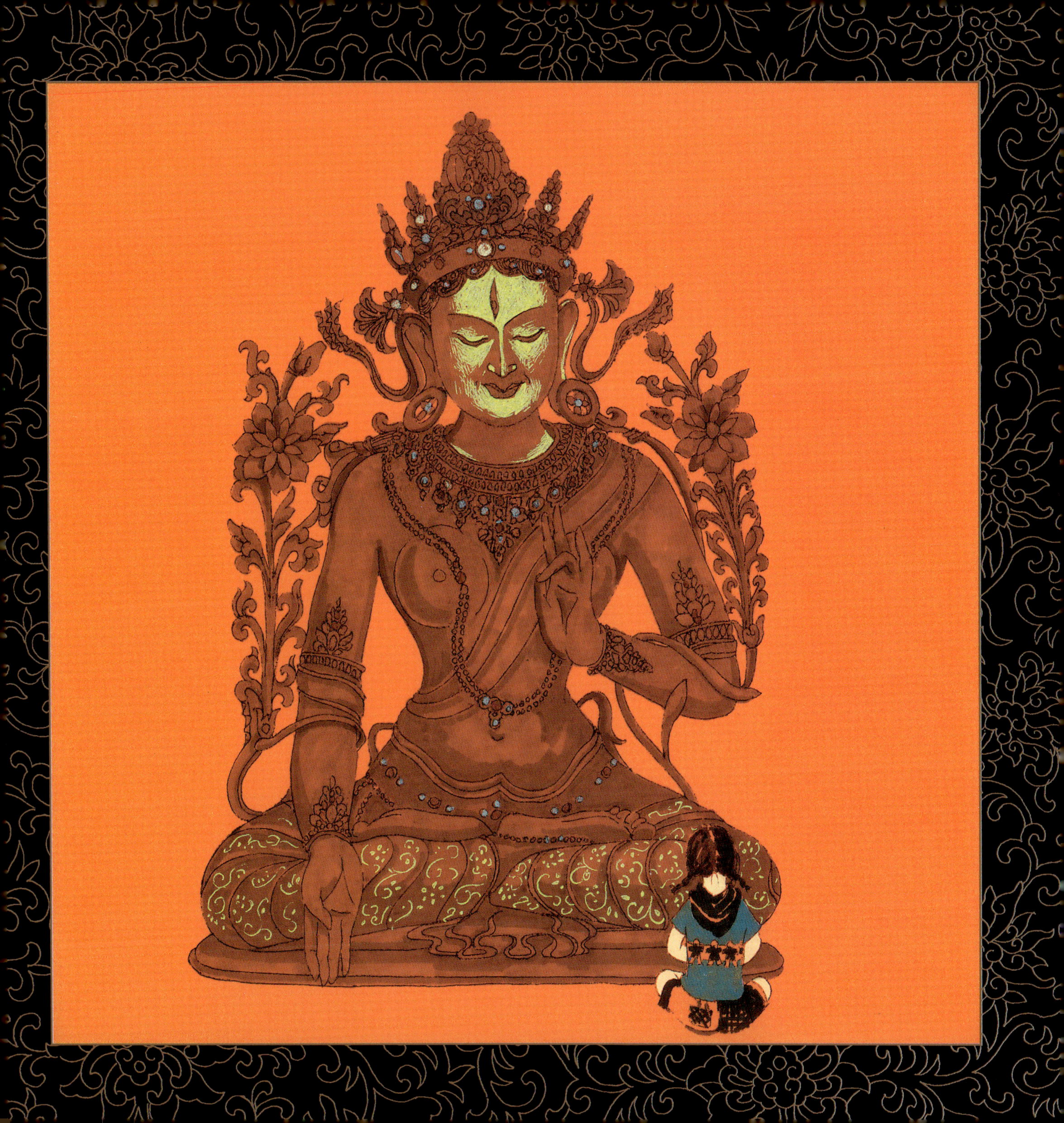

Come, try this machine of mine!

"Do you drink from a feeding bottle?"
"No, I don't. I have eight wet nurses."

"What time of year would it be tonight in the palace on high?"

It is said that this old cypress tree in the palace once died for no apparent reason. During an inspection tour ▷ of the south, Emperor Qianlong found that whenever there was a scorching sun there was a cypress to provide cool shade. Finding that the old cypress tree had revived when he returned to the palace, the emperor believed that the tree had followed him along his tour, so he conferred upon it the title "Marquis Shade."

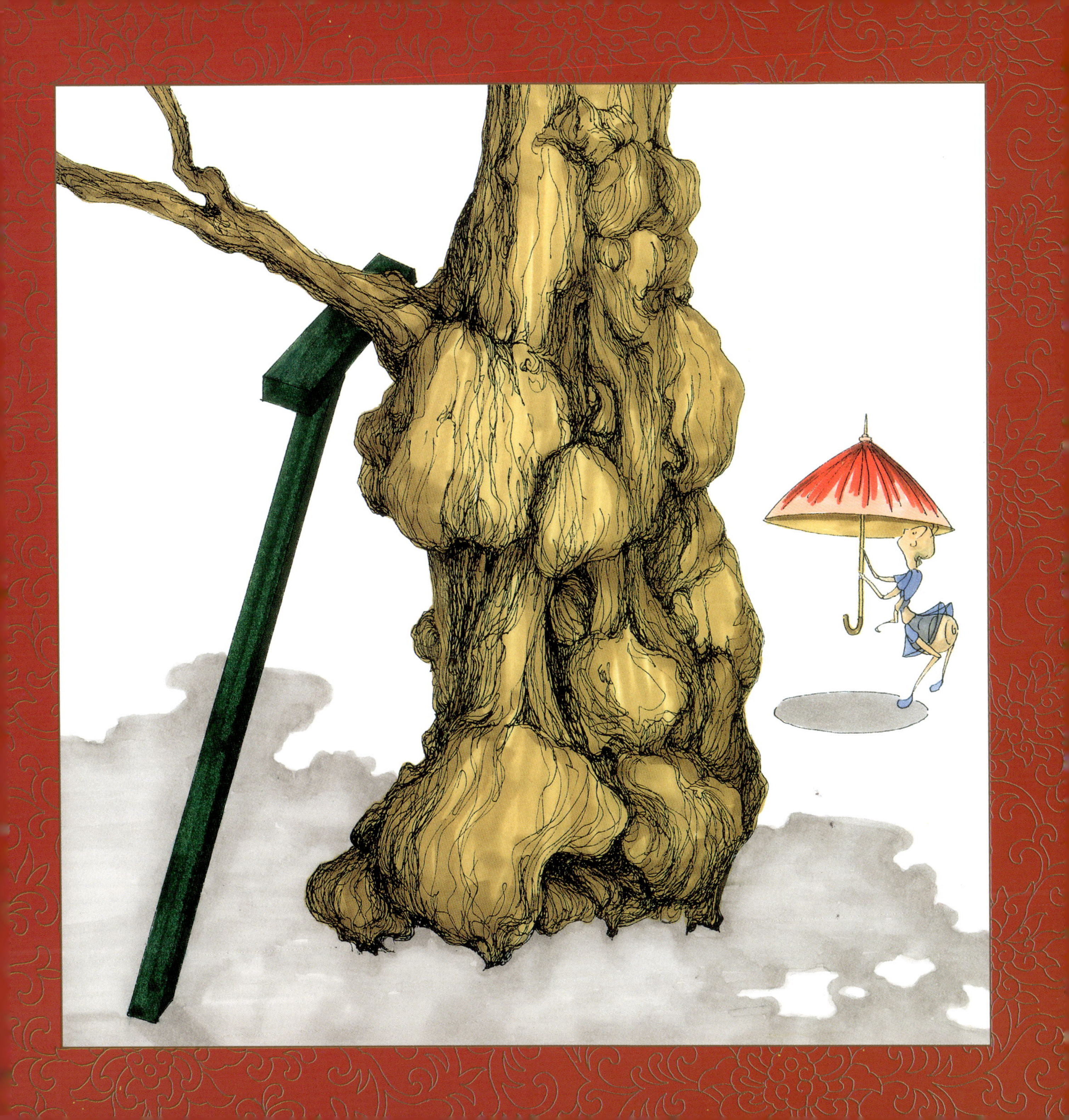

"Congratulations to Worthy Lady Lan." The imperial harem took up a half of this world. It seemed fair that the women's fates were determined by the emperor's choice of whom to spend the night with. They were ranked as Imperial Honored Consort, Imperial Concubine, Worthy Lady....

My memory has faded. Which aria did I sing?
But I clearly remember the favor I received
as the result of my performance.

It is hard to imagine how they spent the long nights without electric lamps, telephones or TV in this immense palace.

One remains a prisoner either within or outside this extraordinarily gorgeous gateway. Perhaps the one within the gateway had more chance to get out of this imprisonment.

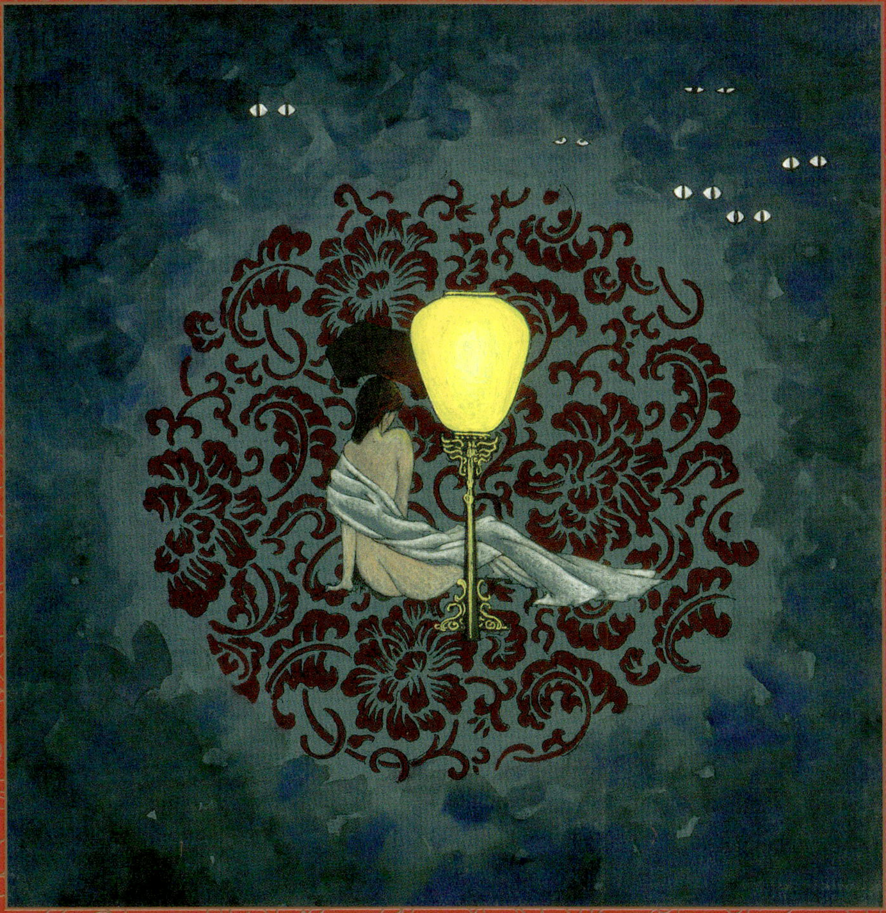

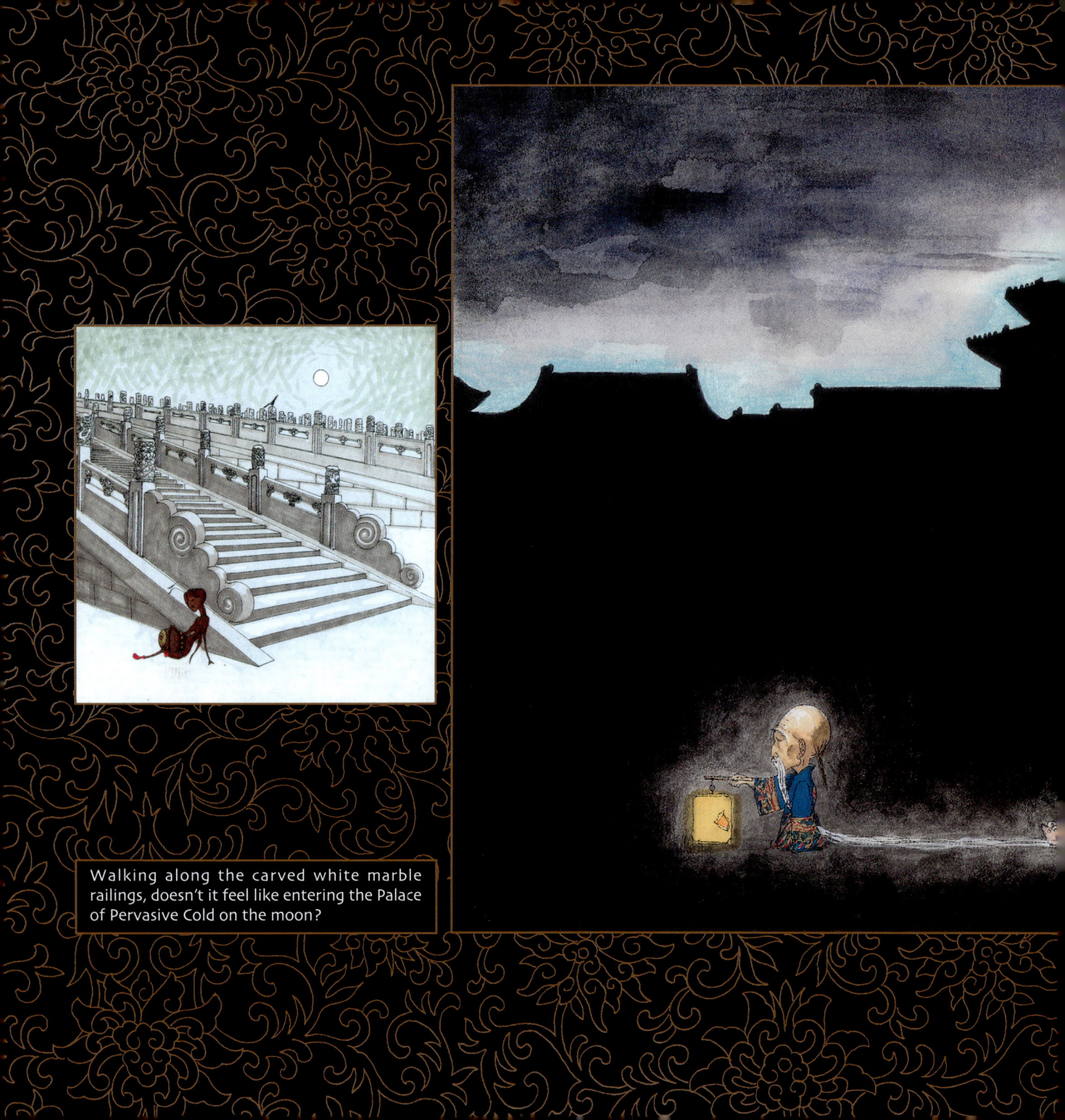

Walking along the carved white marble railings, doesn't it feel like entering the Palace of Pervasive Cold on the moon?

Strolling around the Forbidden City at night, you'll find a different atmosphere. It is said that someone once bumped into an old man with a long white beard. Occasionally you'll hear the night watches, and see the vague shadows of dancing palace women.

In the imperial harem, I've painted quite a number of portraits of imperial concubines, each of which is disappointing. But their looks were not more beautiful than their portraits.

These are the "three-cun lily shoes" in my collection.

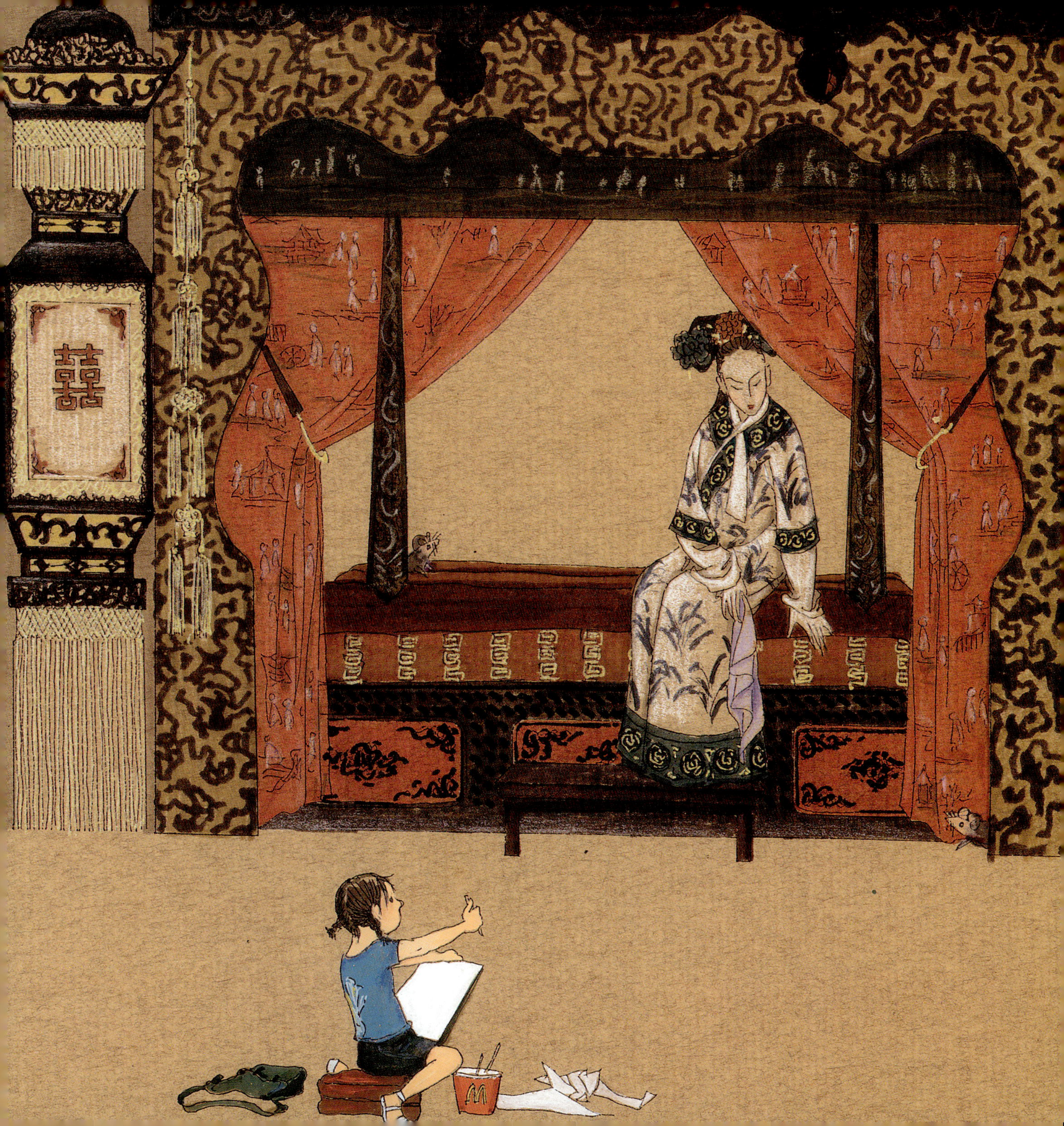
囍

The most beautiful dress in the world should be worn by the most beautiful lady in the world.

Are they unable to bear the sight of it? Or are they pretending they don't see it? Was Imperial Concubine Zhen thinking of the emperor when she was thrown into the well? Look at the miserable eyes of this cat sitting by the well.

I'm having a hard time guarding the city. It was captured not because of the strength of the invaders, but because of the weakness on our side.

My goodness! I don't want to be an imperial concubine!

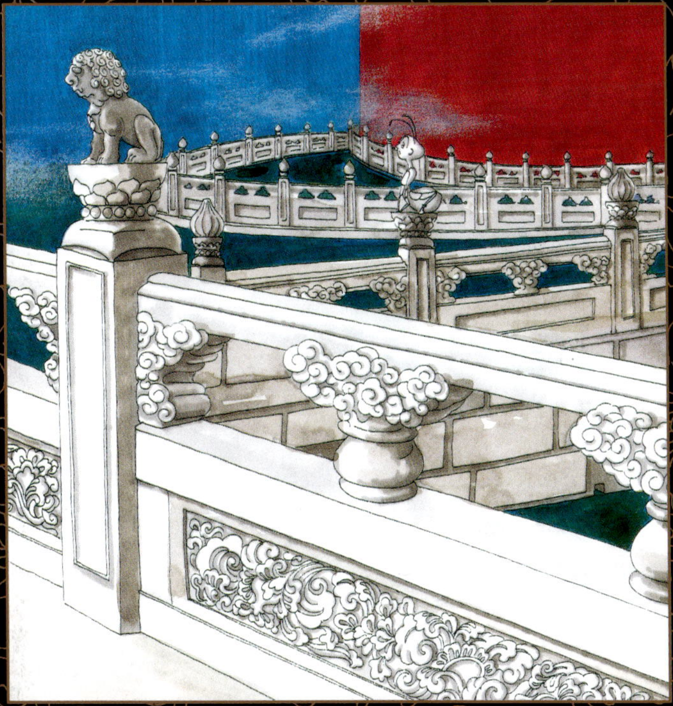

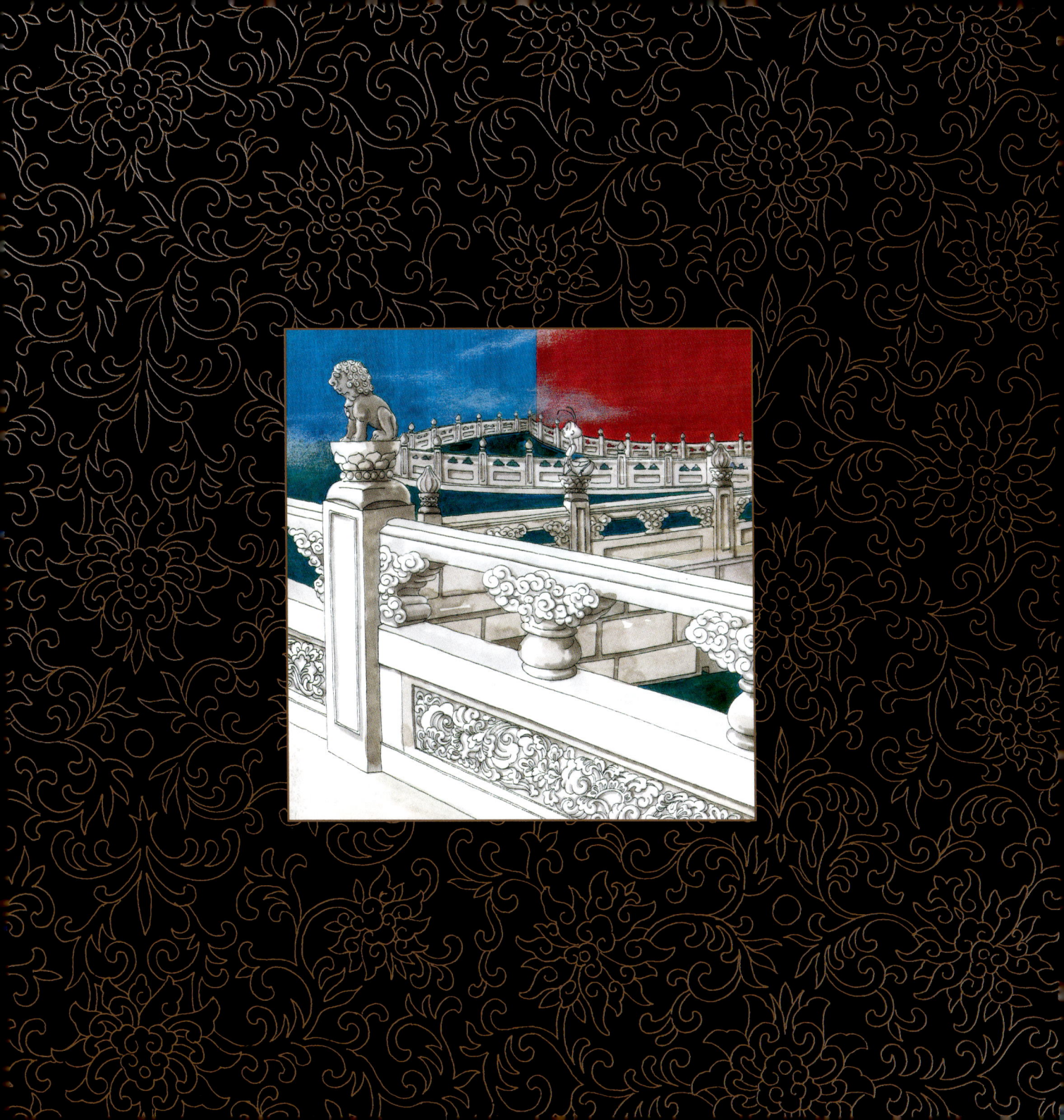

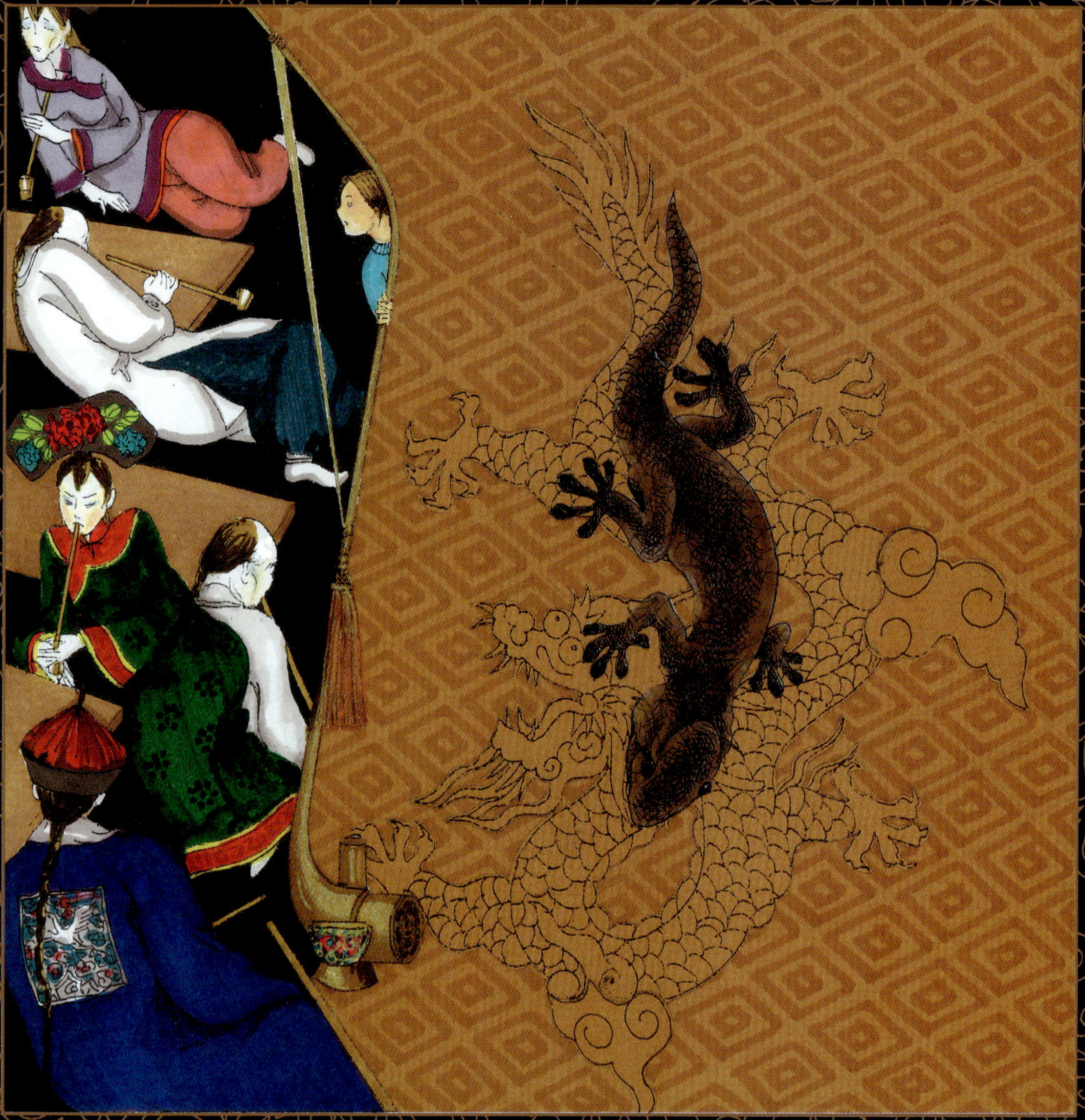

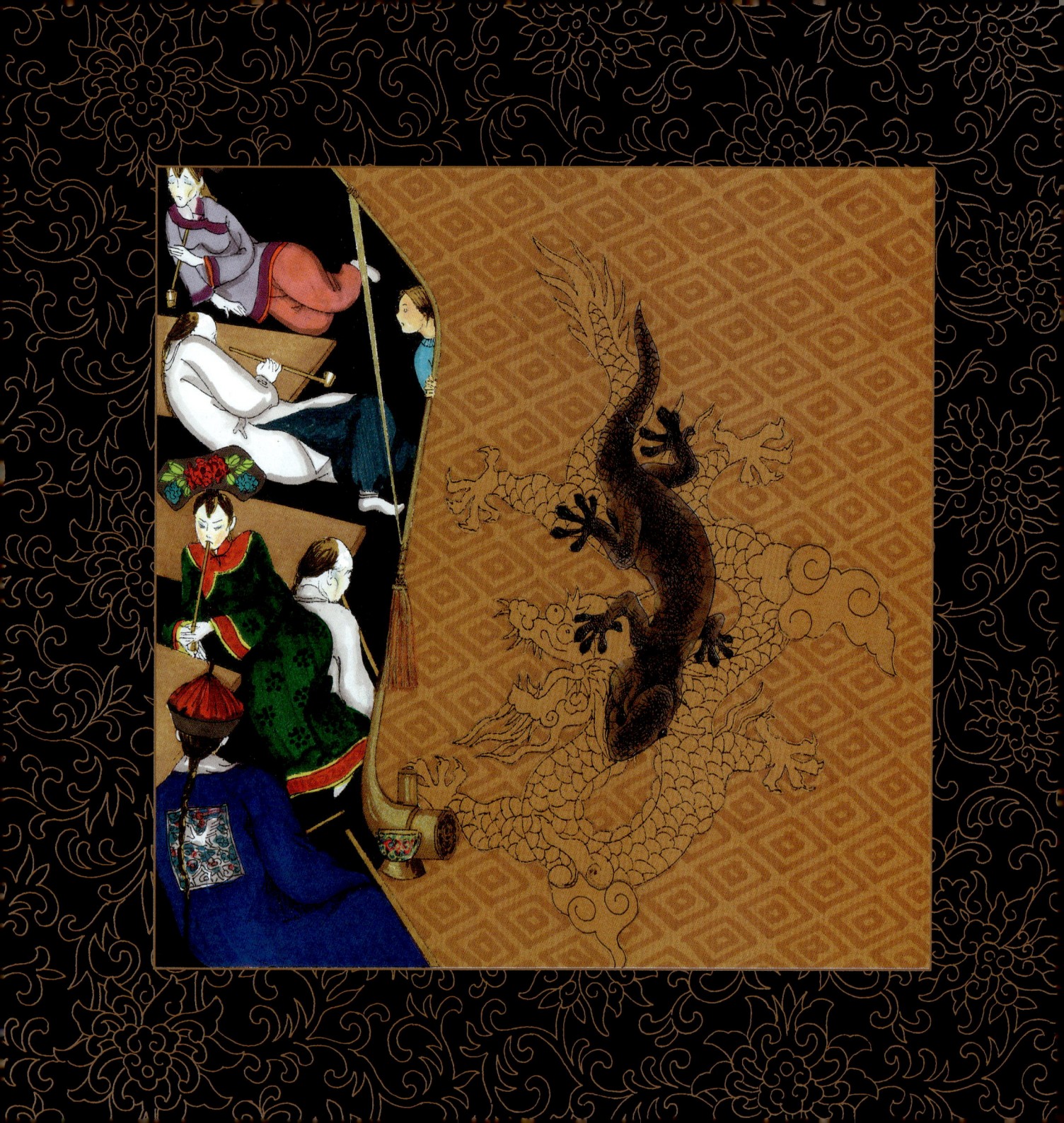

History witnessed each ancestor in power for decades, more than a dozen years, or only a few years.

◁ Once upon a time, the Great Qing Empire was forged by a heroic people through war. But what was once proudly claimed to be the "dragon's spine" was broken by Western cannons and opium.

In a dream, I experienced the moment when the army of the Taiping Heavenly Kingdom broke into the Forbidden City. I escaped by hiding in this big vat.

The peony was a favorite flower of the imperial family, because it looks graceful and splendid with its large corolla.

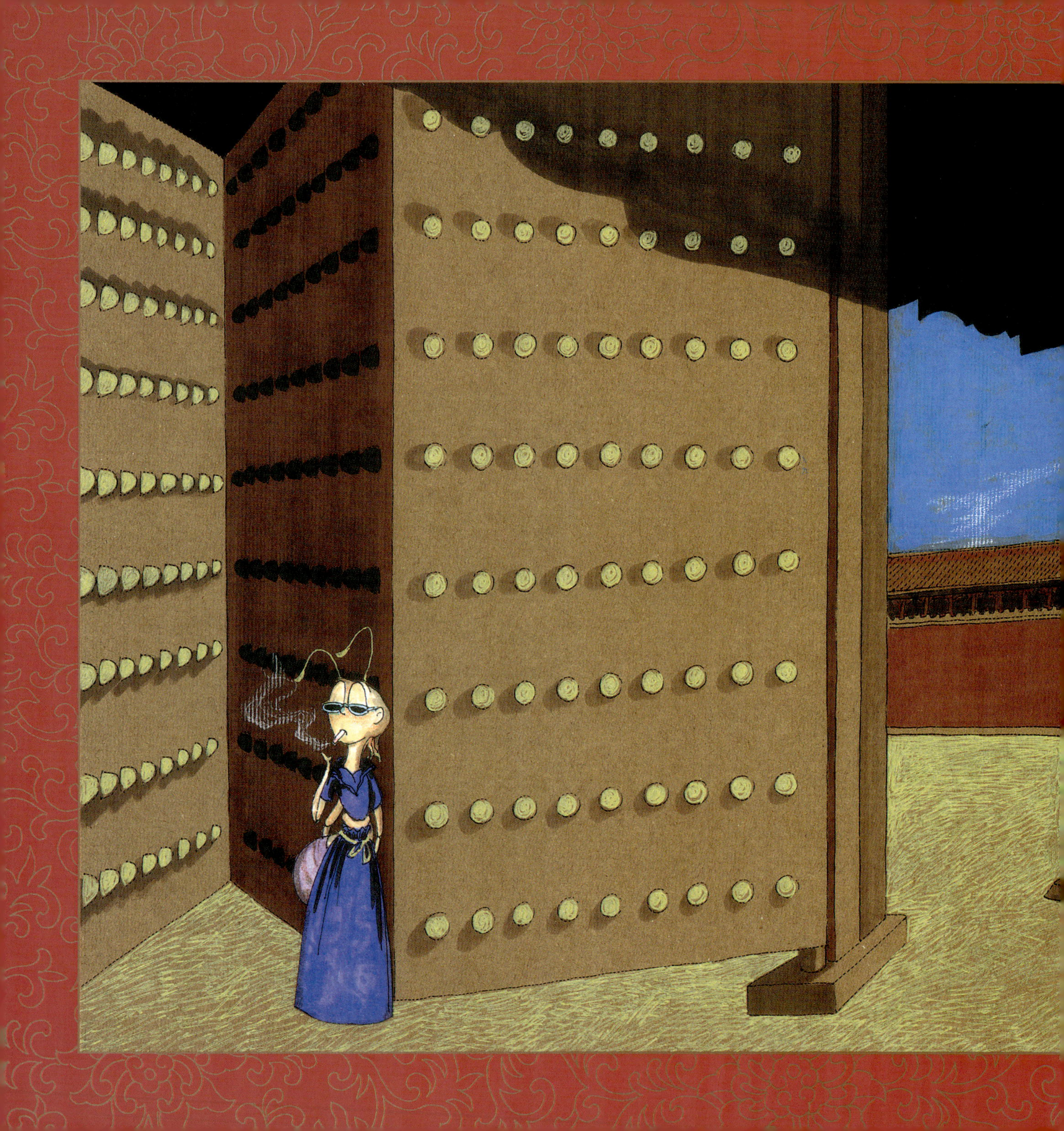

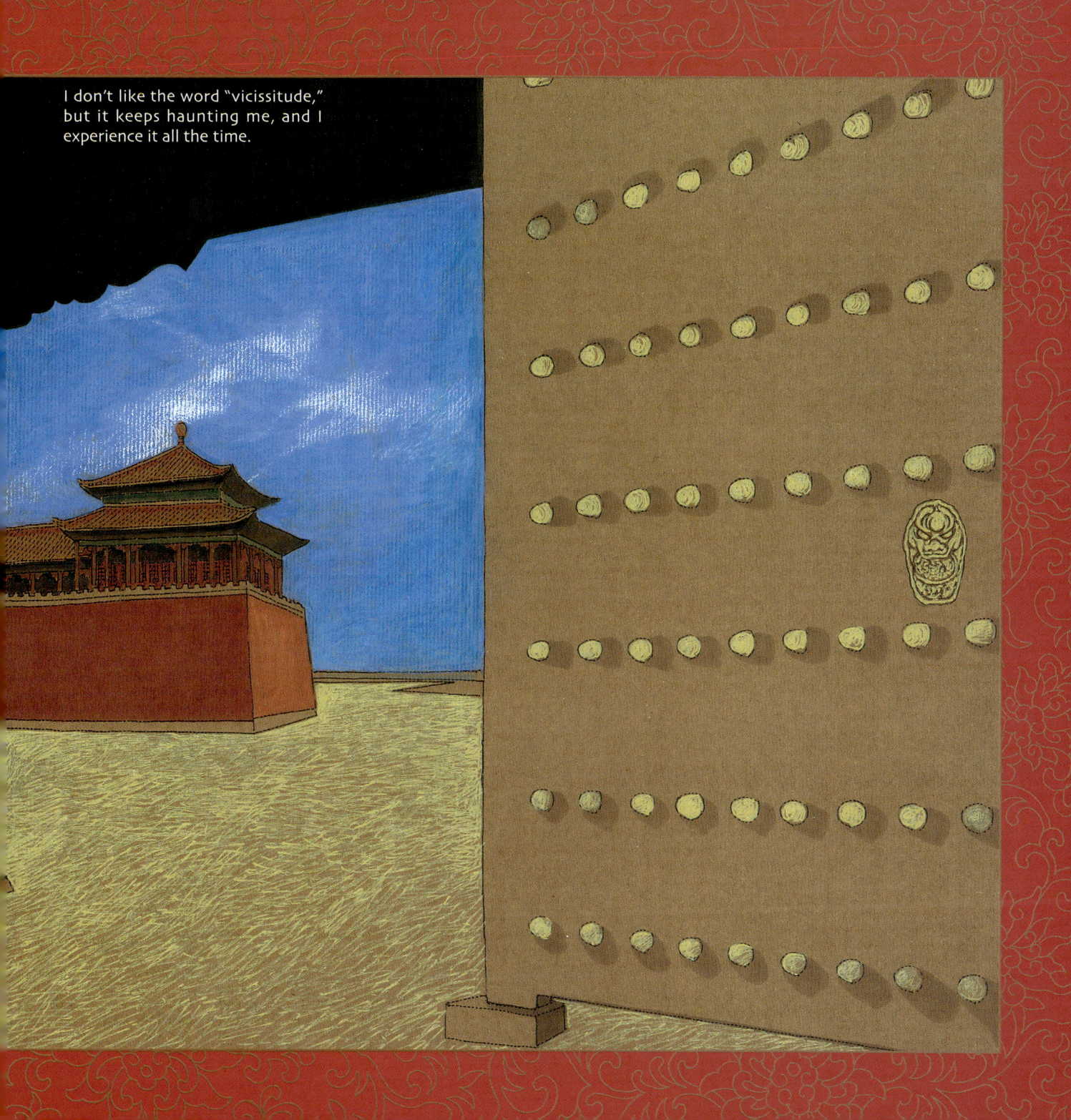

I don't like the word "vicissitude," but it keeps haunting me, and I experience it all the time.

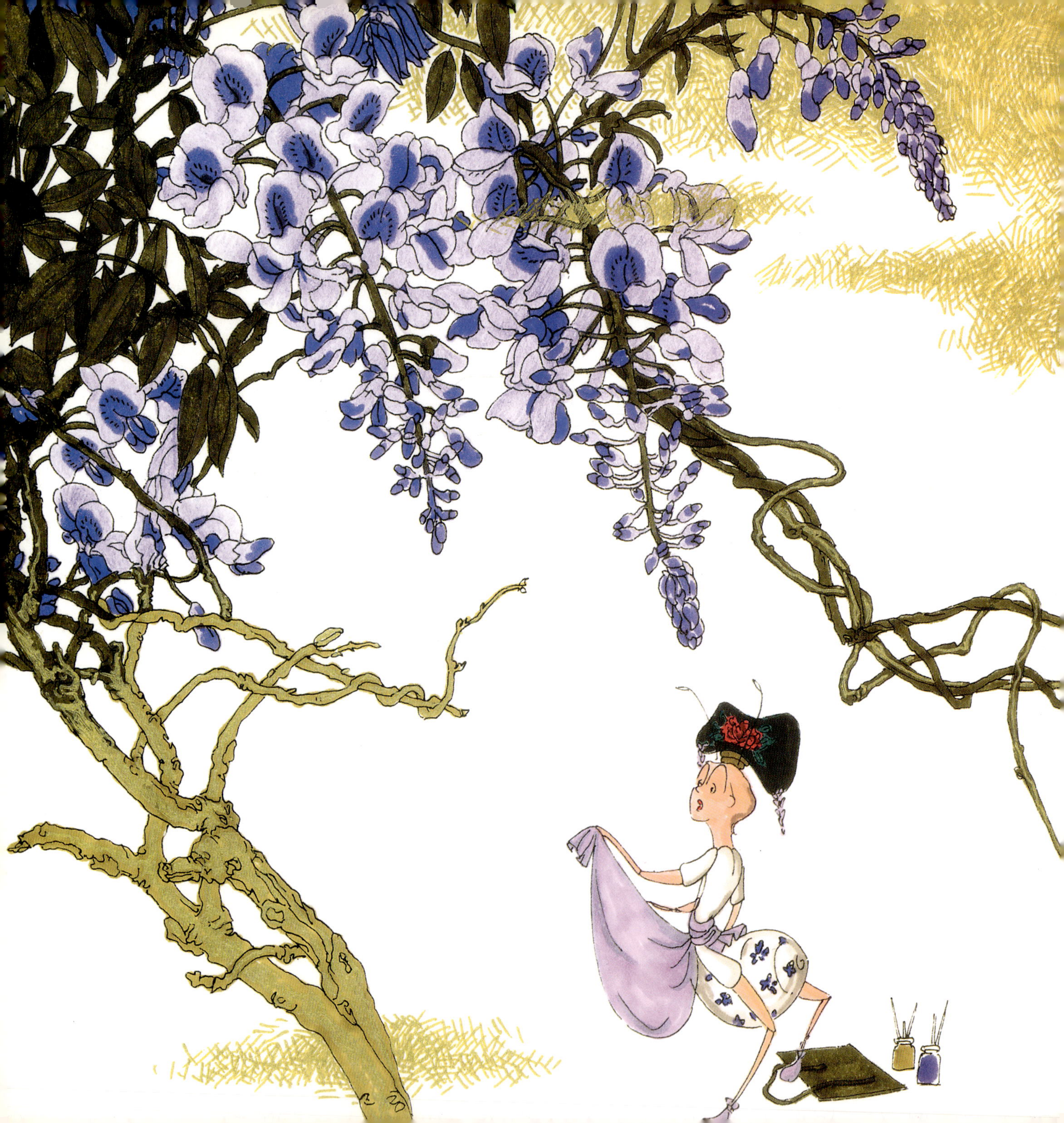

These works of mine were all inspired by the Forbidden City.

◁ I stay in the imperial garden for a few days, imagining how it feels to live like an immortal that eats flowers, drinks dew and soars across the skies on a crane. According to historical records, "The imperial gardens are full of precious stones, verdant trees and vines, which are all several hundred years old."

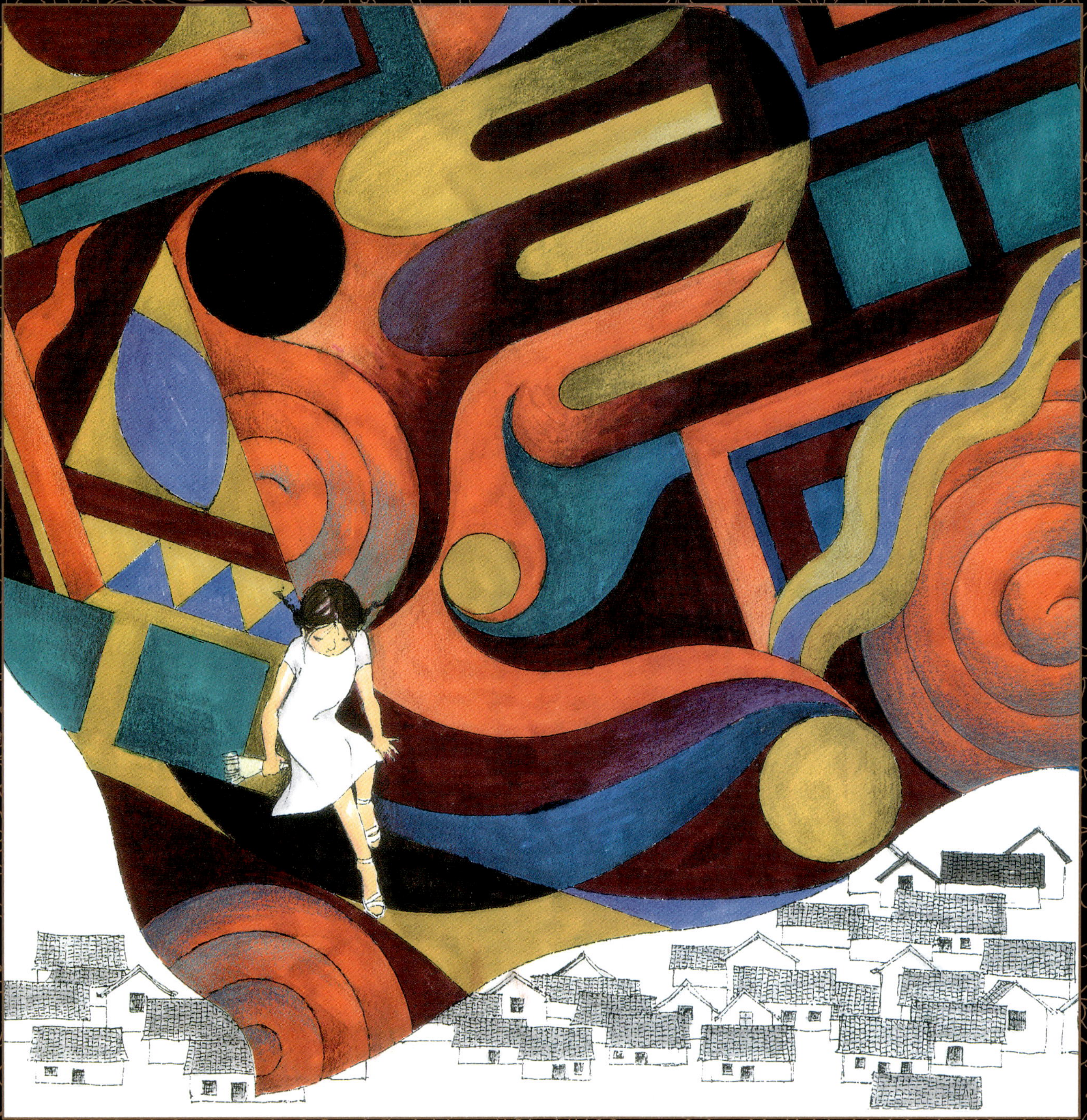

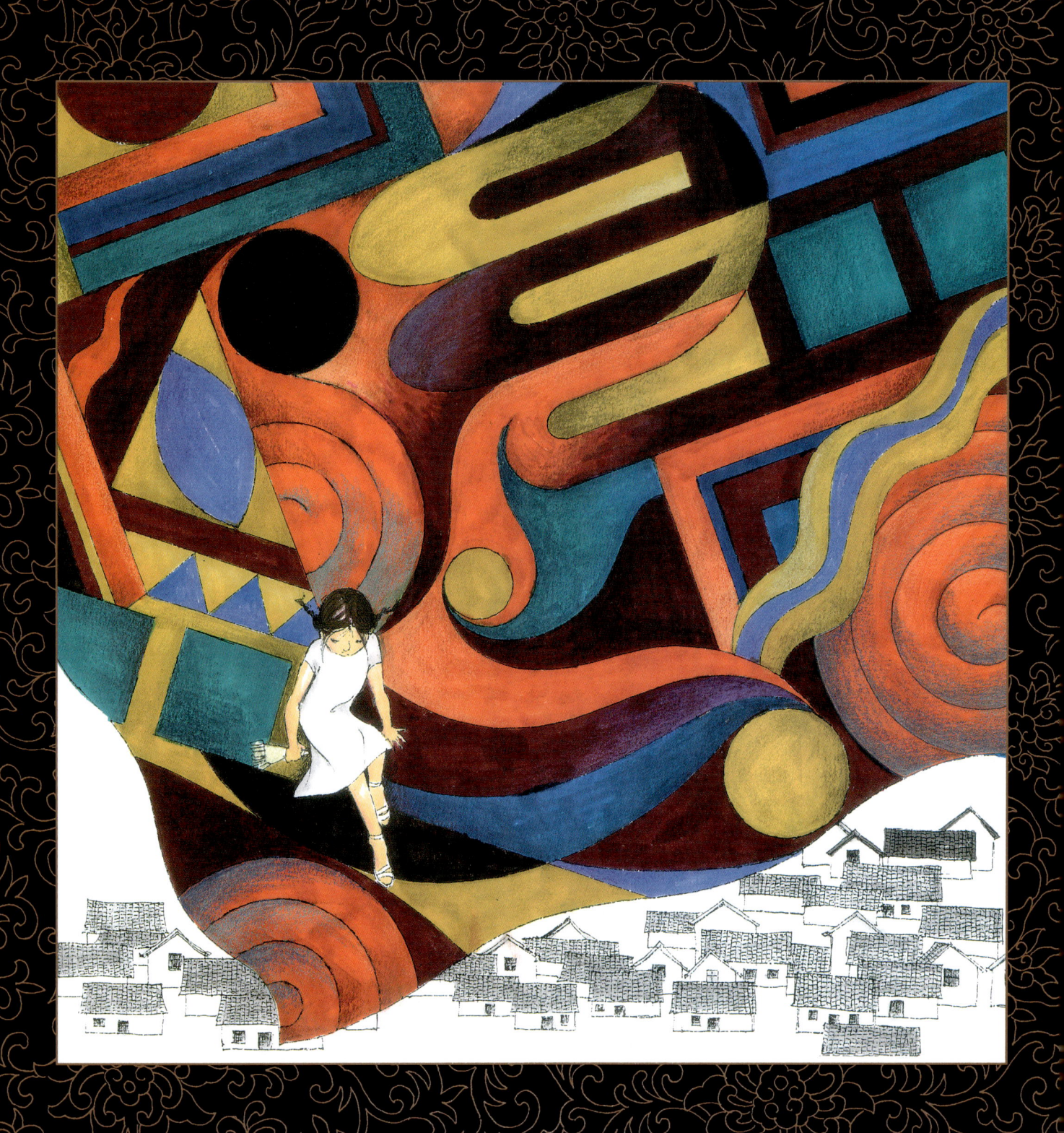

◁ I've brought out all the fascinating colors from the imperial palace, to decorate dreams and brighten each patch of darkness.

The palace has a great collection of treasures from all Chinese dynasties. This is the basis for today's Palace Museum.

The multi-colored glaze forms an admirably harmonious contrast against the red wall. It's like a beautiful, silent symphony, but I can hear it.

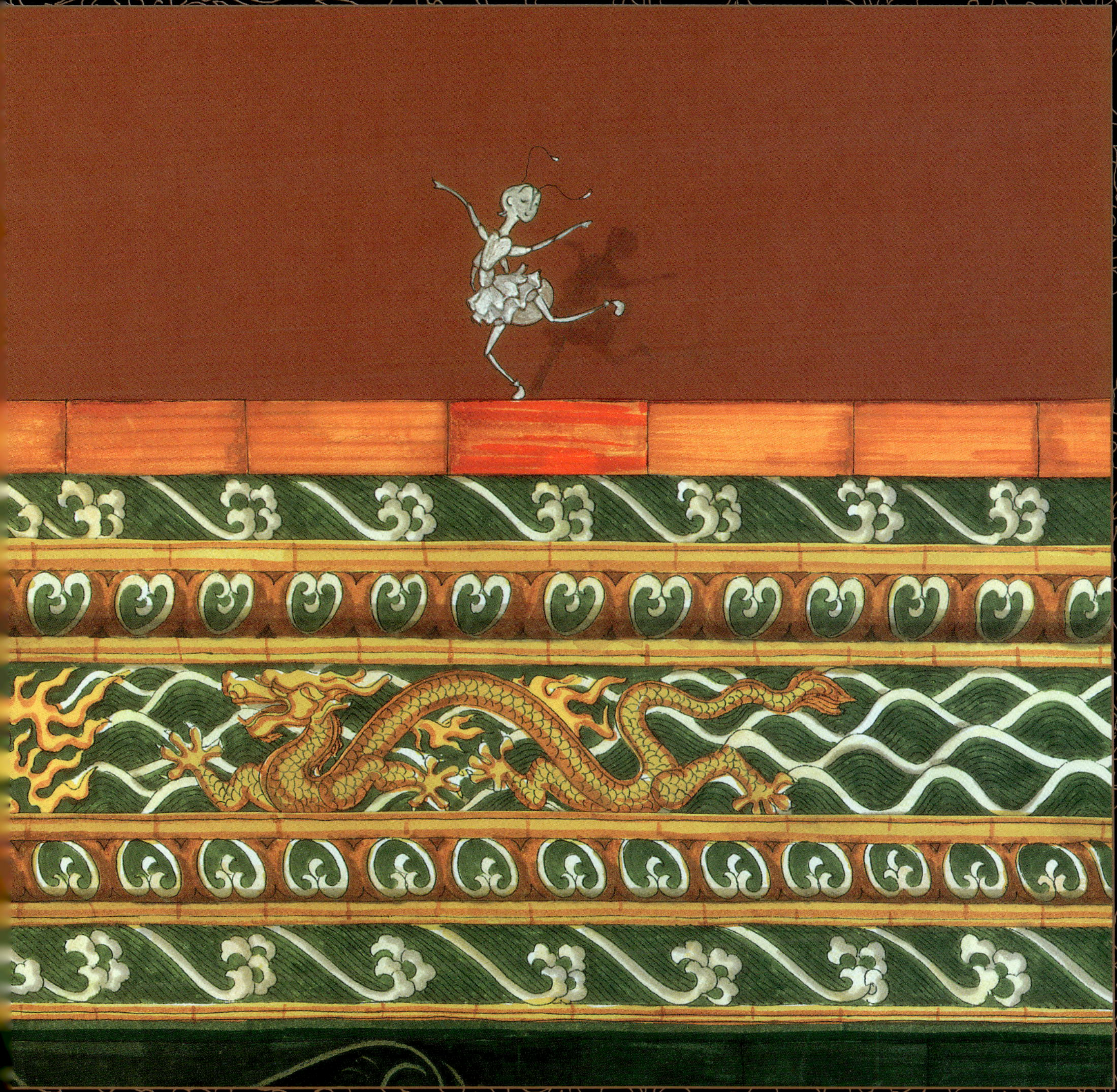

The Thousand-Autumn Pavilion in the imperial garden looks too splendid to be true, like a stage setting.

中国古代天文学将北极星附近的区域分为三垣二十八宿，三垣为紫微垣、太微垣、天市垣，其中紫微垣就是现代天文学中的北极星。古人认为紫微垣是不动的，而所有的群星都在环绕它旋转，所以称之为帝星。紫微星垣，传说就是天帝居住的地方。

人间的帝王是上天的儿子，于是把天子居住的地方叫做紫禁城。

虽说紫禁城坐落在人间，不像天庭那样遥远，但是只因中间的这个"禁"字，也便阻断了一切平民百姓们的遐想。

远远的能望见那红墙，那黄瓦，然而却只能是远远的。甚至不及一只小鸟、一条小虫，可以那般自在无碍地出入。十米高的宫墙、五十二米宽的筒子河将紫禁城圈在当中，这深深的沟壑与高高的屏障挡住了人们好奇的视线，也围起了一片神秘的禁地。

人们在河边遥望着，在墙外谈论着，在心中猜测着，在梦中幻想着，然而小鸟、小虫们却在里面亲见着、亲历着。

真想亲口问问那些小鸟、小虫，它们到底看见了些什么？

皇上凶不凶？

皇后美不美？

宫女苦不苦？

太监坏不坏？

传说永乐年间（1403—1424年），有两件宫中大案株连致死了三千宫妃、宫女。皇上曾亲临刑场，"欣赏"这些弱女子被一一凌迟，这些可怜的女子，她们曾经在紫禁城中怎样地生活过？

嘉庆年间（1796—1820年），皇上迷信道教，以少女炼丹。十六名宫婢不堪其侮，想勒死皇帝，却在慌乱中将绳子打错了结，结果功亏一篑。十六宫婢与受牵连的两名妃嫔，一同被剐。皇帝受惊吓过度，再也不敢在这里居住，因为他觉得"壬寅大变，内有枉者为厉"。二十年后他战战兢兢地回到紫禁城，却在当晚就"驾崩"了。你们可曾看见是谁杀死了他吗？是那些女孩儿的冤魂吗？

1644年，李自成打进北京，绝望的崇祯皇帝（1628—1644年在位）挥剑将自己的妻女杀死"殉国"，在一片尖叫声中残肢短臂横飞，大殿上顿时尸横遍地，血流成河。平白地装点了末世的

列祖列宗，脱下龙袍，披头散发地吊死在了景山的歪脖树上。从此以后，听说那山上往往"鬼哭，天阴则闻"，总有人喊着："群臣误国！"据说就是死去的崇祯。你们可曾见到过他的鬼魂？

传说清初的摄政王多尔衮与顺治皇帝（1644—1661年在位）的母亲孝庄太后是情侣，在宫里如同一家人一样居住，你们见过他们幽会吗？

还有，顺治所深爱着的董鄂妃娘娘她好看吗？她是江南的名妓董小宛吗？她和皇上花前月下的私语你们可曾听见些？

有人研究说，康熙皇帝（1662—1722年在位）的太子像极了《红楼梦》里的宝玉，你们见过他吗？可也是一幅痴痴的相儿？

雍正皇帝（1723—1735年在位）死的时候，真有刺客吗？据说还是个女子，叫吕四娘。

光绪皇帝（1875—1908年在位）到底是不是慈禧害死的？他的珍妃是如何被扔到井里的？那一刻她说了些什么？可曾呼喊过她爱人的名字？

还有，还有好多好多问题……

这样一座已经存在了近六百年的庞大宫殿里，到底发生过多少故事？到底藏着多少秘密？

我们都不知道。

也许曾经飞过这里的小鸟知道；也许曾经爬过这里的小虫知道；也许世代生活在这里的乌鸦们知道，也许出没在荒弃的殿宇间的狐仙知道；也许飘浮在阴暗中的冤魂们知道，也许紫微星垣中的天帝知道。

然而，我们还不知道。

那么，抛开混乱的记载，冲破典籍的迷雾，让紫禁城幻化作斑斓的光影，琢刻成唯美的造型，在我们心里这拳头大小的地方留下这样美好的记忆：你可以自由地搭建，可以随意地着色，可以用梦幻的色彩讲述一段历史，可以用经典的图案诠释一种形象，更可以用柔软的心灵来构建一座属于我们自己的紫禁城。

于是，一切不再遥远，当自己也幻化成这巍峨中的一个小元素的时候，这些故事中也就有了我们的影子。

也能够亲见着，亲历着……

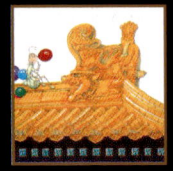

皇帝的家太大了，而我自己渺小得像个小蚂蚁。在这里先后住过明清24位皇帝。

在故宫里许多燕子和麻雀飞来飞去，它们虽不被人驯养，却是这偌大皇宫中最有生命力、最自由的生灵。

何谓正大？何谓光明？正大，而天地之情可见矣；光明，天道下济而光明。"正大光明"正是天帝的德性也。

故宫到底有多大？它是法国卢浮宫的4倍；俄罗斯彼得堡冬宫的9倍；日本东京皇宫的3倍。总之它是最大的，保存最完整的皇家宫殿。

安放在乾清宫台基两侧的镏金铜殿，称社稷江山金殿。"社稷"与"江山"都是国家的代称。放置它们的意思无非是"普天之下莫非王土，率土之滨莫非王臣"。

谁见过1,142个螭首同时吐出如柱的雨水，名副其实的千龙吐水的壮观景象啊！

由屋檐到横梁之间那些结构复杂的拼木构成的斜面，叫斗拱。据说是运用杠杆与天平原理设计而成的，叫人看得眼花缭乱。

我一直想看清楚那大殿顶端的"吻兽"到底是什么样子，有可能的话，把我的气球放到上面去。

支撑着天的红漆大柱,其实并非根根都是如此粗实的圆木,不少是拼出来的,它们的周长是3.15米。

门,使我们与另外一个时空产生了障碍,而故宫的门便是天堂与人间的界碑。故宫的大门上有横9排、竖9排,共81个门钉。在中国民间"9"数代表最大。

你为什么轰我们,这难道不是我们的家吗?看那墙上的图案分明是我们的专利。

想从这里爬上天,谈何容易。孰不知,你已经在天上了。

紫禁城名称的由来,要到天上的紫微宫去找个说法。

日晷玉盘上均匀地刻出24条时刻线,晷针则随着太阳的移动而移动,这恐怕是最早的时钟了,真太聪明了。

不知此为何物的大有人在,这是明清时期宫内插灯杆用的灯杆座。每逢上灯时典礼还非常隆重:"不夜城,灯月高,奉辰欢,暮暮朝朝。"

我喜欢这儿的每个角落,因为每个角落都是一幅画。墙上的装饰、房檐上的瓦当,路上的拼花,我都不愿忽略了它们。

传说故宫有9,999.5间房子，因为天上玉帝的天宫有10,000间，皇帝虽贵为天子，但不能超越天制，只好少建半间。实际上故宫共有房间8,707间。

我的这件作品叫《不透气的天空》，因为它不是我画的，老师该如何给先人们打分呢？

"我欲乘风归去"，是它的企盼吗？如果是，它为何久立于此500年。它的企盼真是我们的愿望吗？

这九龙壁可不只是有前壁后壁18条龙，仔细寻找会有惊人的发现：上面大大小小共有635条龙。

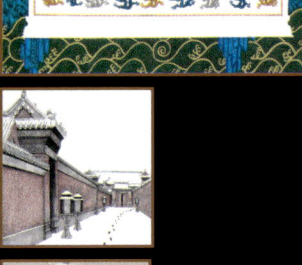

紫禁城的建筑是对称的，有左翼门，就有右翼门，有中左门，就有中右门……你看到了这条西长街了吧，跟我再去看看东长街。

"宫殿像'天宫仙阙'，虽天上之清都，海上之蓬瀛，犹不足以喻其境也……。"

故宫是个神秘的地方,当你跨进故宫的大门,需要像历史学家那样思考，像美学家那样凝望……

你听见雄狮在发出阵阵低沉的怒吼吗？这似乎与黄河的澎湃涛声是一个节拍。在这里它们被禁锢着、压制着。

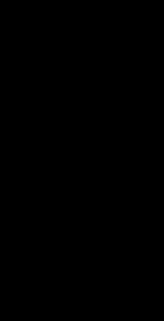

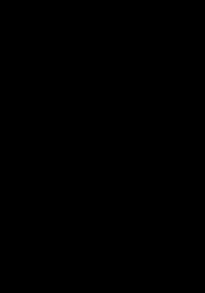

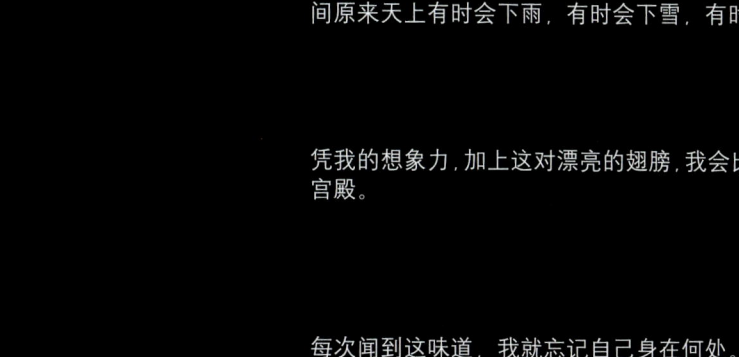

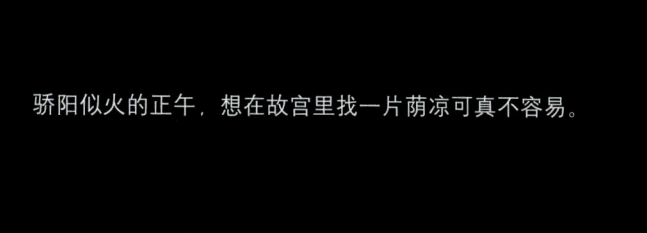

故宫的几座大殿,金銮殿最雄伟,中和殿最郁闷,保和殿最亲和。三个大殿被重重叠叠的廊庑环绕着,如同浮在云层之上。三大殿四周没有一棵树,据说是怕有人藏于树丛中对皇帝构成威胁。

真正的武林高手在皇帝的身后,他们的兵器就藏在羽扇之中。皇帝宝座下也有一把匕首以备不测。

骄阳似火的正午,想在故宫里找一片荫凉可真不容易。

午门前一直是封建统治阶级举行"献俘"仪式的场所,明清两代自不例外。明代还在午门前举行一种特殊的刑罚——廷杖。同时它还是一个兵械库,也像博物馆,陈列着开国先帝的丰功伟绩。

我告诉你:"这座宫殿始建于15世纪初期,那时正是明朝永乐皇帝时代。是1406年下"诏书"筹建,用了十余年的时间,到1420年主要建筑完成。"你可以去告诉别人。

尽管我看不到天的全部,头顶这片蓝色却给了我足够的放飞想像的空间原来天上有时会下雨,有时会下雪,有时还会下树叶。

凭我的想象力,加上这对漂亮的翅膀,我会比宇航员更先见到天上的宫殿。

每次闻到这味道,我就忘记自己身在何处。

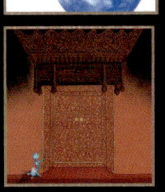

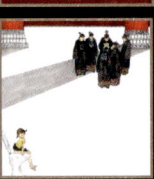

在故宫里"龙"是主宰，这是个不可思议的符号。但每个黄皮肤的中国人，无论走到天涯海角，却心甘情愿被它"缠绕"，臣服于它的力量，直到今天。

皇帝议政时坐的龙椅叫金銮宝座，是天下最大的、最至高无上的东西了。

在故宫众多的门中，有屋宇门、牌坊门、垂花门……这叫毗卢帽垂花门，是连亲王都不准受用的，是皇帝专用的门式。真是太牛了！

皇帝住在一间没有电器设备的房间里。如果有电视机或电子游戏机的话，他也不用备三宫六院七十二嫔妃了。

"膳齐"，开始奏乐，皇帝在太监簇拥下走向膳桌用膳。实际上皇帝吃不了几品菜，剩下的大部分赏赐嫔妃和大臣了。

"嘘，小点声儿，皇帝睡觉啦！"

关注皇帝的健康，不只是太医院的事，而是每个臣子的事，这可是关系着江山社稷的头等大事。

你知道为什么故宫许多大门没有门槛吗？是末代小皇帝为自己骑自行车方便，命人把它们都拆掉了。

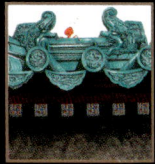

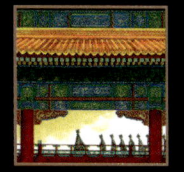

这些稀罕玩意儿，是行贿皇帝的礼物。

皇子、皇孙上学的地方叫"上书院"，就设在乾清宫内。离皇帝住处近，也便于皇帝随时督查。他们四五岁便进了上书院，直到封爵、另立王府或别有任命才离开。因为是皇子、皇孙呆的地方，所以房顶是绿瓦。

我确信皇宫中孩童的生活绝对没有我们过得开心。这儿的一切都太过神圣，还有点神秘，以致让人感到惶恐。

人们不是说：天无二日吗？

故宫本身就像个大戏台，漂亮精美的布景，离奇、荒诞的故事，以及神秘兮兮的人物。

宫中有种极可悲又极可憎的无性人——太监。

明朝皇帝宠爱太监，宫中共养太监10万人。乾隆时期宫中有太监2600名，直至八国联军攻打北京时宫内太监减至2000人。

这里除了威严、还有阴谋，并在迅速的蔓延……因为这巨大的宫殿阳光无法照进来。

我曾拥有过喝斥别人的权利吗？

乾隆皇帝的母亲在过60岁生日时，乾隆为之建万佛楼，有佛龛一万，并命京师王公大臣及外省大吏，各献金佛像一尊，来填补空缺……于是，开始了百姓得孝敬官僚、官僚要孝敬皇上、皇上再孝敬娘亲、娘亲却孝敬佛祖，而佛祖的心中只有众生。

"来，看我的。"

"你用奶瓶吗？"
"不用，我有八个乳娘。"

"问天上宫阙今昔是何年？"

传说这棵老树曾一度无疾而终。但乾隆南巡途中，每当烈日当空，便有一棵柏树像伞盖一样为他撒下清荫。当乾隆回宫后发现这枯死的古柏又复活时，皇帝确信它正是为他护驾的柏树，于是赐封它为"遮荫侯"。

"恭喜兰贵人！"
后宫是这世界的另一半，要靠皇帝翻牌来决定这些女人的命运似乎也公平。在她们中有明显的等级差别，皇妃、嫔妃、贵人……

我的记忆已经模糊不清了，我是演唱了哪个段子？但由此受宠的结果，我确清楚的记得。

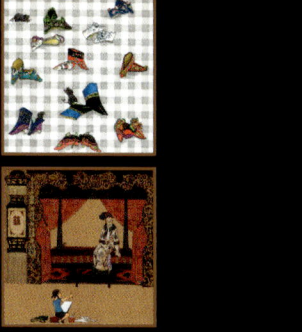

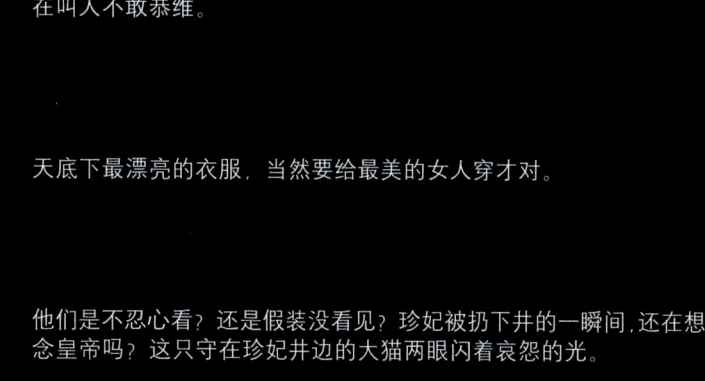

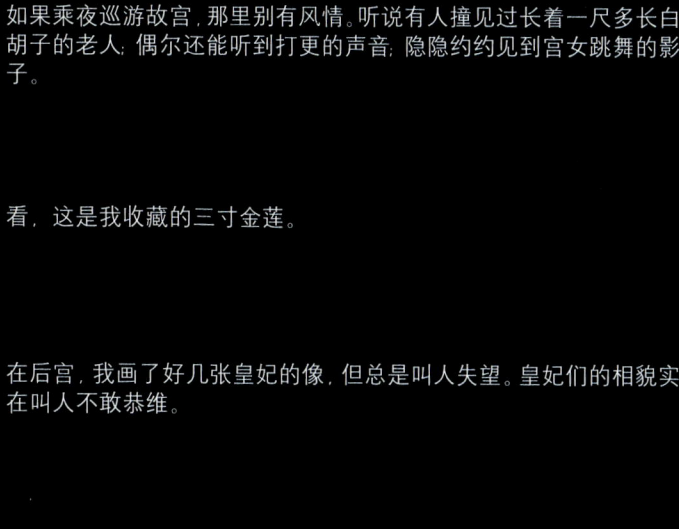

在这华美异常的门里、门外，都是一样被囚禁。或许在门里出头的机会还大一点，

偌大的宫殿，夜晚没有电灯、电话，没有电视，难以想像她们是如何度过这漫漫长夜。

沿着这白玉雕栏登上重重叠叠的石阶，像不像进入中国民间描述的月亮上的广寒宫？

如果乘夜巡游故宫，那里别有风情。听说有人撞见过长着一尺多长白胡子的老人；偶尔还能听到打更的声音；隐隐约约见到宫女跳舞的影子。

看，这是我收藏的三寸金莲。

在后宫，我画了好几张皇妃的像，但总是叫人失望。皇妃们的相貌实在叫人不敢恭维。

天底下最漂亮的衣服，当然要给最美的女人穿才对。

他们是不忍心看？还是假装没看见？珍妃被扔下井的一瞬间，还在想念皇帝吗？这只守在珍妃井边的大猫两眼闪着哀怨的光。

"哎哟妈呀！我可不想当皇妃了。"

嘿，看见我了吗？
我在这儿护城如此辛苦。落日失守，不是因为外部的强大，而是我们内部的渺小。

曾几何时，大清帝国也是靠铁骑弯刀打天下的英雄民族。不料洋炮加烟枪却打软了自称龙的脊梁。

列祖列宗各领风骚几十年、十几年、几年。

我曾梦见自己亲历了李自成的农民军打进这座紫禁城的情景，是这口大缸让我逃过一劫。

牡丹之所以受皇家宠爱，因其花冠硕大，且雍容华贵，富丽堂皇。

我不喜欢"沧桑"，但我无法摆脱这两个字的缠绕，而且每时每刻都深深地体验着它。

我在御花园一呆就是几天，体会着食花饮露，乘鹤云游般神仙的感觉。史书上说："御花园内珍石罗布，嘉木郁葱，又有古柏藤萝，皆数百年物。"

看我的这些作品,灵感全部来自故宫。

我把宫中那令人痴迷的色彩带出来,点染梦中的故事,撒给每一片灰暗。

这儿有太多的宝贝,历代珍品这里都有,所以后人把这儿叫做《故宫博物院》。

琉璃的缤纷色彩与红墙平分秋色。我赞叹这对比所产生的和谐,美丽如同无声的交响乐。当然,我能听到!

这坐落在御花园内的"千秋亭",像是舞台剧中的场景,艳丽得有些不真实。

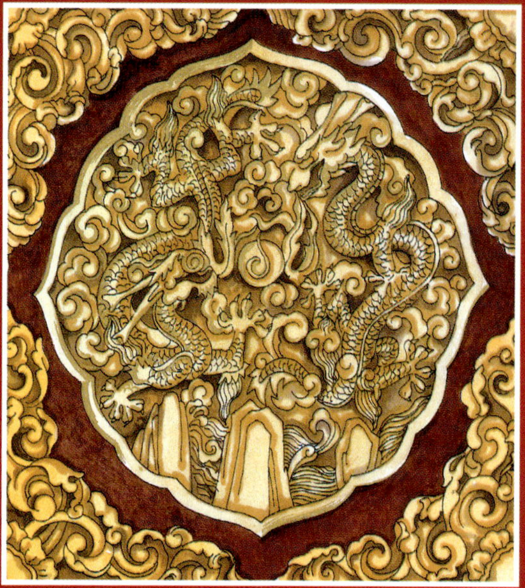

图书在版编目（CIP）数据

魂游故宫／羊子编绘．－北京：外文出版社，2005．
ISBN 7-119-03900-8

Ⅰ．魂… Ⅱ．羊… Ⅲ．故宫-概况-英、汉 Ⅳ．K928．74

中国版本图书馆CIP数据核字(2004)第138569号

编　　绘：羊　子
责 任 编 辑：兰佩瑾
翻　　译：张韶宁
英 文 编 辑：郁　苓
设　　计：元　青 等
封 面 设 计：兰佩瑾

魂游故宫

© 外文出版社
外文出版社出版
（中国北京百万庄大街24号）
邮政编码：100037
外文出版社网页：http://www.flp.com.cn
外文出版社电子邮件地址：info@flp.com.cn
sales@flp.com.cn

天时印刷（深圳）有限公司印刷
中国国际图书贸易总公司发行
（中国北京车公庄西路35号）
北京邮政信箱第399号　邮政编码100044
2005年(20开)第1版
2005年第1版第1次印刷
（英汉）
ISBN 7-119-03900-8
07800（平）
85-EC-547P